The Trans-Atlantic Slave Trade

A Database on CD-Rom

Edited by

David Eltis
Stephen D. Behrendt
David Richardson
Herbert S. Klein

CAMBRIDGE
UNIVERSITY PRESS

PUBLISHED BY THE PRESS SYNDICATE OF THE UNIVERSITY OF CAMBRIDGE
The Pitt Building, Trumpington Street, Cambridge, United Kingdom

CAMBRIDGE UNIVERSITY PRESS
The Edinburgh Building, Cambridge CB2 2RU, UK   http://www.cup.cam.ac.uk
40 West 20th Street, New York, NY 10011-4211, USA   http://www.cup.org
10 Stamford Road, Oakleigh, Melbourne 3166, Australia
Ruiz de Alarcón 13, 28014 Madrid, Spain

First published 1999

Printed in the United States of America

Typeface: AGaramond

Library of Congress Cataloging in Publication data is available.

A catalog record for this book is available from the British Library.

ISBN   0 521 62910 1 CD-ROM

Contents

How to Use This CD-Rom

THE HOME SCREEN:

The Home Screen is the main screen with navigational buttons to all areas on the CD-ROM. Click the "Home" button to return to the Home Screen.

THE QUERY SCREEN:

The Query Screen allows for the input of custom and predefined queries of the Slave Trade Database. Click the "Query" button to go to the Query Screen.

NOTE: When entering the Query Screen for the first time, all the voyages are displayed

PERFORMING A QUERY:

1. Once in the Query Screen, **select the time period** to be queried from the time period drop-down menu. If a specific time period is selected (other than "Full time period") a second time period drop-down menu appears. Select the specific time period from this secondary drop-down menu.
2. **Select the region to be queried.** Select the region parameters from the first region drop-down menu (select the blank if you do not wish to constrain your query by a specific region), then select the region name in the second region drop-down menu.

3. **Select query filters.** Select your first query filter in the first drop-down menu. Select an operator ("<", "=", or ">") in the second drop-down menu. With some filters, a list of filter parameters is generated in the third drop-down menu from which you can select. If this is not the case, then input your own filter parameter. For assistance in defining appropriate filter parameters you may wish to view the Codebook. If more than one filter is desired, select a Boolean operator ("AND" or "OR") in the fourth drop-down menu and select additional filters as described above.

   NOTE: Queries are cASe sEnsiTive!!

4. **Perform Query.** Once all Query parameters have been selected, click on the "Perform Query" button. Once your query is performed the Query Results are displayed in the lower half of the screen.

CUSTOMIZING THE QUERY DISPLAY AREA:

DISPLAY AREA HEIGHT:

1. Roll the mouse over the horizontal screen divider right above the Query Results area.
2. When the cursor changes to the double-arrow adjuster click and hold the mouse button down.
3. Slide the horizontal divider up or down.

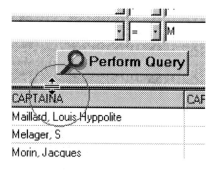

COLUMN WIDTH:

1. Roll the mouse over the vertical divider line between two column headers.
2. When the cursor changes to the double-arrow adjuster click and hold the mouse button down.
3. Slide the vertical divider left or right.

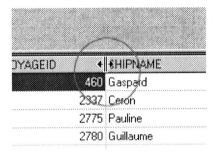

COLUMN ORDER:

1. To change the column order, click and hold down the mouse button on the column header.
2. Slide the column left or right and release the mouse.

ACCESSING VOYAGE DETAILS FROM THE QUERY DISPLAY:

1. Highlight any cell in the row of the voyage you wish to review.
2. Double-click on the row or column header to view the voyage details.

VIEWING VOYAGE DETAILS:

1. Double-click on any cell in the Query Results area to view a complete table of voyage details

SAVING AND LOADING QUERIES:

SAVING A QUERY:

1. Click the "Save. . ." button.
2. Input a name for the current query and press "OK".

LOADING A SAVED QUERY:

1. Click the "Load. . . " button.
2. Select a query from the list by clicking on it an press "OK".
3. The name of the query appears in the upper-right corner of the screen

DELETING A SAVED QUERY:

1. Click the "Load. . . " button.
2. Select a query from the list by clicking on it and press "Delete".

RENAMING A SAVED QUERY:

1. Load a saved query.
2. Click the "Save As. . . " button.
3. Input a name for the current query and press "OK".

QUERY ANALYSIS:

1. After performing a query, click the "Analysis" button.
2. Once the Analysis Screen is in view, use the "Print" or "Copy" button to print or copy the table.

QUERY SUMMARY:

1. After performing a query, click the "Summary" button.
2. Once the Summary Screen is in view, use the "Print" or "Copy" button to print or copy the table.

QUERY GRAPH:

1. After performing a query, use the drop-down arrow button to the right of the "Graph" button to select "Embarkations" or "Disembarkations," then click the "Graph" button.
2. Once the Graph screen is in view, use the "Print" or "Copy" button to print or copy the graph.

ZOOMING IN ON A GRAPH:

1. The graph Zoom-in feature allows a closer look at any rectangular region of the graph.
2. Click and hold down the mouse button on any corner of the region you wish to zoom in on.
3. While still holding down the mouse button, drag the mouse to the diagonally opposite corner of the region on which you wish to zoom in and release the mouse button.
4. Click the "Zoom out" button to restore the graph.

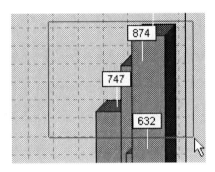

PANNING ACROSS A GRAPH:

1. Click and hold the right mouse button down.
2. Move the mouse to pan across the graph.

QUERY MAP:

1. After performing a query click the "Map" button.
2. Once the Map Screen is in view, use the "Print" or "Copy" button to print or copy the map.

ZOOMING IN ON THE MAP:

1. The map Zoom-in feature allows a closer look at any rectangular region of the map.
2. Click the "Zoom in" button.
3. Click and hold down the mouse button on any corner of the region you wish to zoom in on.

4. While still holding down the mouse button, drag the mouse to the diagonally opposite corner of the region on which you wish to zoom in and release the mouse.
5. Click the "Zoom out" button to restore the map.

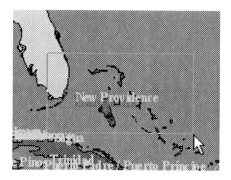

PANNING ACROSS THE MAP:

1. Click and hold the right mouse button down.
2. Move the mouse to pan across the map.

SHOWING/HIDING PORTS ON THE MAP:

1. Click the "Show Ports" check box to view the ports on the map.
2. Click the "Show Ports" check box again to hide the ports on the map.

PRINTING AND COPYING DATA:

1. Use the "Copy" button to copy data from the Analysis, Graph, Map, or Summary screens. NOTE: The Analysis and Summary screens are copied as text and the Graph and Map screens are copied as bitmaps.
2. Use the right mouse button to copy highlighted text or a specific cell in the Query Screen grid.
3. Use Ctrl-V to paste the selected text into your program.
4. Use the "Print" button to print data from the Analysis, Graph, Map, or Summary screens. Use the "Set Up Printer" button to set your printer settings and the "OK" button to commence printing.

THE SLAVE TRADE CODEBOOK:

The Codebook is a lookup table containing all the names and descriptions of the fields within the database. The Codebook is useful in creating Query filters.

In the format column of the Codebook, "A" refers to "Alphanumeric", so "A40" means the field is a 40-character string. "F" refers to "Float", so "F4" means the field is a real number with 4 digits and "F6.4" means the field is a real number with 6 digits to the left of the decimal point and 4 to the right.

THE SLAVE TRADE METHODOLOGY:

The Slave Trade Methodology contains information about the database, sources, and data variables. To locate the full version of the abbreviated information source provided in variables SOURCEA through to SOURCER, use the "Find" button in Methodology and type in the first several letters of the abbreviation.

DOWNLOADING THE SPSS DATA FILES:

Copies of the SPSS formatted databases are located on the CD in the folder called "SPSSDATA". Use the SPSS application (not included with this CD-ROM) to open file D:\SPSSDATA\COLE4.SAV" (where "D" is the drive letter of your CD-ROM drive).

INTRODUCTION

David Eltis, Stephen D. Behrendt, David Richardson, Herbert S. Klein

It is difficult to believe that at the dawn of the twenty-first century that just over two centuries ago, for those Europeans who thought about the issue, the shipping of enslaved Africans across the Atlantic was morally indistinguishable from shipping textiles, wheat, or even sugar. Our reconstruction of a major part of this migration experience covers an era in which there was massive technological change (steamers were among the last slave ships), as well as very dramatic shifts in perceptions of good and evil.[1] Just as important perhaps were the relations between the Western and non-Western worlds that the trade both reflected and encapsulated. Slaves constituted the most important reason for contact between Europeans and Africans for nearly two centuries. The shipment of slaves from Africa was related to the demographic disaster consequent to the meeting of Europeans and Amerindians, which greatly reduced the numbers of Amerindian laborers and raised the demand for labor drawn from elsewhere, particularly Africa. As Europeans colonized the Americas, a steady stream of European peoples migrated to the Americas between 1492 and the early nineteenth century. But what is often overlooked is that, before 1820, perhaps three times as many enslaved Africans crossed the Atlantic as Europeans. This was the largest transoceanic migration of a people until that day, and it provided the Americas with a crucial labor force for their own economic development. The slave trade is thus a vital part of the history of some millions of Africans and their descendants who helped shape the modern Americas culturally as well as in the material sense.

   Those using this data set should recognize certain basic limitations. The data set contains thousands of names of shipowners and ship captains, but it contains no names of the millions of slaves carried to the Americas. Thus, anyone seeking genealogical information on Africans or Afro-Americans can use these data only indirectly to locate the African origins of groups of slaves arriving in America at a given time and a given place. The data set may, however, be combined with other sources that do provide names. In Latin America it was more common to list last names of slaves, usually indicating their African national identity as well as could be done. In fact, most African historians have had to rely on Latin American lists for getting at national origins of the Africans who were forced to migrate. Thus, plantation records, church records of vital statistics (births, marriages, deaths, baptisms, and confirmations), along with judicial and military records, can be used to get lists of names. In the North American case, it was uncommon to list last names, and planta-tion records, except in rare circumstances, only give first names. For example, names of slaves never appear in the United States Federal Census.

Although of limited utility for persons seeking their own family histories, our data set does provide an extraordinary source for historical reconstruction of the his-tory of the African peoples in America. These 27,233 voyages will enable historians to develop new insights into the history of peoples of African descent and the forces that determined their forced migration. The voyages greatly facilitate the study of cultural, demographic, and economic change in the Atlantic world from the late six-teenth to the mid-nineteenth centuries. Trends and cycles in the flow of African cap-tives from specific coastal outlets[2] should provide scholars with new, basic informa-tion useful in examining the relationships among slaving, warfare—in both Africa and Europe—political instability, and climatic and ecological change, among other forces. The data set should provide new impetus to assessments of the volume and demographic structure of the trans-Atlantic slave trade. Though the shipping records employed in creating this data set do not include specific information on the ethnicities of African peoples,[3] annual (or monthly) coastal migration data from the voyage data set will nonetheless allow African historians to bring to light the slaving pathways from the interior to the coast. With more precise data on the African ori-gins of slaves in the Americas, scholars will be able to better assess patterns of cul-tural retention and adaptation. Moreover, the ways in which Africans shaped the At-lantic world—through agricultural innovations, belief systems, patterns of vital rates, and a variety of cultural practices—will be brought into sharper focus.[4] Slave ship insurrections are flagged in the data set so that the study of African agency through resistance to the trade is now placed on a systematic footing for the first time. For European societies located on either side of the Atlantic, the data set con-tains new information on ship construction and registration and relatively extensive records of owners' and captains' names. It will now be easier to pursue connections between the slave trade and other sectors of European and American economies. Re-searchers should be able to unravel trends in long-distance shipping activities, par-ticularly important because no comparable body of data exists for other transoceanic trades. Data on crew mortality are abundant. The implications for new assessments of the social as well as the economic role of the slave trade in the regions where the slave voyage originated are obvious. In short, the major aim of our project at the Du Bois Institute is to facilitate and stimulate new research on the slave trade, the impli-cations of which reach far beyond the slave trade itself.

If these grand hopes are to be realized, researchers will need to know the prove-nance, structure, and sources of the data set, the better to assess what questions it may be used to address. A glance at the appendix of sources establishes the data set as being the product of an international research endeavor that has ranged far beyond the labors of the current authors. From the late 1960s, Herbert S. Klein and other scholars began to collect archival data on slave-trading voyages from unpublished sources and to code them into a machine-readable format.[5] In the 1970s and 1980s, scholars created a number of slave ship data sets, several of which the current authors have chosen to recode from the primary sources rather than integrate into the present set. By the late 1980s, there were approximately 11,000 individual trans-Atlantic voyages in sixteen separate data sets, not all of which were trans-Atlantic, nor even slave voyages, nor, indeed, were the data without overlap. In addition, several listings of voyages extracted from more than one source had appeared in hard copy form, notably three volumes of voyages from French ports published by Jean Mettas and Serge and Michèle Daget and two volumes of Bristol voyages (expanded to four by 1996) authored by David Richardson.[6] The basis for each data set was usually the records of a specific European nation or the particular port where slaving voyages originated, with the information available reflecting the nature of the records that had survived rather than the structure of the voyage itself. Scholars of the slave trade spent the first quarter century of the computer era working largely in isolation, each using one source only as well as a separate format, though the Curtin, Mettas, and Richardson collections were early exceptions to this pattern. Voyage records combining data from several national or port archives were unusual.

The idea of creating a single multisource data set of trans-Atlantic slave voyages emerged from a chance meeting of two of the authors (David Eltis and Stephen Behrendt) in the British Public Record Office in 1990 while they were working independently on the early and late British slave trades. At about the same time a third author, David Richardson, was taking over detailed multisource work on the large mid-eighteenth-century Liverpool shipping business begun years earlier by Maurice Schofield.[7] All this work, together with the Bristol volumes already published, made it seem feasible to integrate the records for the very large British slave trade for the first time, and beyond that, given the available Dutch, French, and Portuguese data, to collect a single data set for the trade as a whole. In January 1991 the idea of a consolidated data set of trans-Atlantic voyages was discussed at an informal gathering at the annual meeting of the American Historical Association. Barbara Solow suggested seeking sponsorship from the W. E. B. Du Bois Institute for Afro-American Research at Harvard University, headed by Professor Henry L. Gates, Jr. At the initiative of Barbara Solow and Randall Burkett, meetings were held at the Du Bois Institute in 1992 to discuss a grant proposal to be submitted to major funding agencies. In July 1993 the project received funding from the National Endowment for the Humanities with supplementary support coming from the Mellon Foundation. These, with additional funds from the Ford Foundation, allowed six months' leave for two of the principals to complete the project.

By the time the project began, Johannes Postma's Dutch data had become available, as had Stephen Behrendt's compilation of the extensive British trade after 1784, and also the large and complex Richardson, Beedham, and Schofield pre-1787 Liverpool Plantation Register data set, all in machine-readable format.[8] Quantities of smaller sets of published material available only in hard-copy form had been available for some time,[9] and scholars volunteered unpublished data as awareness of the project increased.[10] In the course of the next three years, the project undertook three major tasks. The first was standardizing the existing data. Pioneers in the field had collected their data using different definitions of variables, sometimes of apparently similar items of information, as well as a range of organizational formats (for example using ship-based rather than voyage-based data). The second task was collating voyages which appeared in several different sets, converting single-source data sets into multisource equivalents and even checking on the validity of old compilations.[11] The third task, which became increasingly important as the project progressed, was adding new information.[12] New voyages—new in the sense that they have not appeared in any other published compilation—account for about half of the data presented here. They are mainly voyages from Brazilian, British, and Spanish ports. But in addition to this, our research has added new information to about one third of the voyages already available in existing data sets. Much of the supplementary information is British in origin, but it needs to be stressed that given the ubiquitous nature of British trading, and later, abolitionist interests, non-British voyages are very well represented in these sources. For international coverage, there is simply no non-British counterpart to the *Lloyd's Lists*, a shipping newspaper of the eighteenth century, or, in the nineteenth century, to the correspondence of the network of British Foreign Office observers that is to be found in the FO 84 series of the British Public Record Office.[13]

What is the outcome of this collaboration? It is probable that our data set now includes more than 90 percent of all voyages that left British ports—and the British were the second largest of the national slave trader groups. The data on the eighteenth-century French and Dutch slave trades are also largely complete. The reasons for this are fairly obvious. Compared with other slave traders, northwestern European trading nations conducted the great bulk of their business relatively late in the slave trade era when everyone kept better records. Surviving sources in these countries are therefore abundant. Casual inspection of the relevant variables in our data set shows that almost all the voyages leaving ports in these countries have more than one source of information, and some have as many as eighteen. In the last six months of the project, the editors added *Lloyd's Lists* to the set—as noted already, the most comprehensive information source on shipping movements in the eighteenth century. This shipping gazette provided a rich haul of additional information, but added only 393 new voyages to a set, which, at that stage, contained 11,200 voyages for the years that *Lloyd's Lists* covered. Many of these additional voyages sailed from North American ports where the coverage of the set is less strong. *Lloyd's Lists* generated only two voyages that were not already in the Mettas-Daget compilation and only six new voyages from Dutch ports.[14] New information will certainly emerge on these trades, but we think it unlikely that this will generate many new voyages. There are, of course, numerous slave voyages that are not included in the data set. The Portuguese trade (based largely in Brazil) has the largest gaps, and the nineteenth-century Spanish traffic is also incompletely represented. Much of the seventeenth-century French traffic is missing.[15] Similarly, the minor traders, including the Danish, and the slave trade from colonial North America and U.S. ports—each perhaps no more than 5 percent of the trans-Atlantic trade—are clearly underrepresented. Nonetheless, our set of voyages provides samples large enough to present the major trends over time in the history of the trans-Atlantic slave trade.

Discussion of the representativeness of Iberian, North American, and Scandinavian ships presented here and—given the previous comments—what the set implies about the total size of the slave trade is reserved for another occasion. Most users, however, will wish to have some idea of how complete the set is compared to previous assessments of the volume of the trade. Two widely-cited surveys of the size and direction of the trade, reviewing work published since Curtin's 1969 *Census*, appeared in 1982 and 1989.[16] Broadly, these suggested modest increases in Curtin's estimate of the overall volume of the trade, though more substantial changes in Curtin's temporal and geographic distribution of that overall figure, to 12 million departures from Africa and 10.5 million arrivals in the various reception zones. It should be noted that these estimates include trade to some areas, particularly the Mascarene Islands, that the Du Bois Institute data set does not purport to cover. If we exclude these areas then what we might call the scholarly consensus figures would be 11.8 million departures and 10.3 million arrivals. If we further exclude voyages setting out before 1600—on the basis that the Du Bois Institute set contains only a few such ships—then the consensus figures would be 11.4 million departing and 10 million arriving.[17] In the present set, the average number of slaves on board a slave ship as it left Africa was 332.0; an average of 281.1 per ship arrived in the Americas.[18] Division of these averages into the aforementioned "consensus" aggregates suggests a total of between 34,482 voyages based on numbers leaving Africa and 35,561 voyages based on numbers disembarking slaves.[19]

Our database contains 27,233 voyages that set out to obtain slaves for the Americas. Of these, 2,788 voyages disappeared from the historical record without leaving any information on their activities after departure from their port of origin, and 1,404 voyages failed to embark slaves because of capture or shipwreck prior to reaching Africa. Of the 23,040 expeditions known to have embarked some slaves, 145 sank with the loss of all Africans on board, 1,559 left no information on the subsequent outcome of the voyage, and 607 voyages disembarked their slaves in the Old World. The latter group comprised mainly ships captured in the nineteenth century which were taken to Sierra Leone and St. Helena as part of the attempt to suppress the trade. The new slave trade data set thus contains 20,729 voyages which disembarked slaves in the Americas, and 2,788 voyages which might have reached a destination, but about which we have no further information. This yields a total of 25,076 voyages that did land or could have landed slaves in the Americas. Compared to the estimated total of 35,561 slave voyages arriving in the Americas (see above), this suggests that the data set contains more than two-thirds of all trans-Atlantic slaving voyages which we know obtained some slaves. On the African side, the data set contains 23,040 voyages which we know obtained at least some slaves from

Africa. If we add to these the 2,788 voyages of unknown outcome that could have left with slaves, then we have 25,828 or just under three-quarters of the total number of 34,482 voyages obtaining slaves in Africa. From this perspective the Du Bois Institute data set contains between two-thirds and three-quarters of all trans-Atlantic slave voyages sailing after 1600. Of course, other estimates of the trade exist. If we take a higher estimate of, say, 15.4 million departures,[20] then the ratio falls to about 58 percent. The most recent estimate of the magnitude of the slave trade suggests a small downward revision, and this implies a small proportionate increase in the sample size of our set.[21]

NATURE OF SOURCES

Much of what is new in this data set lies in the sources, which call for some discussion. The published data draw on a wide range of published and archival information. Postma, Mettas, and Richardson used new material in the preparation of their published lists of voyages. Our data set does not reproduce all the sources that previous authors used and listed. Thus, voyages drawn from published sources are represented here by that single reference. Anyone wishing to consult the archival references will have to resort to the hard copy. Editing of this published record occurred only when we found new documentary evidence to support a change and only these new sources are listed separately. Pulling together the results of work carried out in separate national archives was particularly fruitful because trans-Atlantic slave vessels could clear from one jurisdiction and arrive in the Americas in another. Specifically, the international nature of the slave trade meant that a voyage that might appear primarily in one national body of records had a very good chance of showing up, in addition, in the records of other countries. Thus, voyages organized by London merchants operating independently of the Royal African Company (RAC) in the 1670s and 1680s obtained their slaves in South-east Africa, outside the RAC's English monopoly and where the English East India Company had little physical presence. Because almost all these ships called at the Cape before beginning their trans-Atlantic journeys, several of them appear in the Dutch Cape of Good Hope archives.[22] Portuguese ships leaving Bahia in Brazil for the "Mina" coast appear in English Cape Coast Castle material at the Public Record Office. Slave ships of every nationality appear in the *Lloyd's Lists*, and of course the hundreds of slave ships captured in the many European wars are often carefully documented in the archives of the captors, as well as in the records of the nations to which the ships belonged. Indeed, the South Atlantic Portuguese trade remains by far the worst recorded precisely because this branch of the traffic operated to some extent independently of the others. Winds and ocean currents kept the South Atlantic trade out of the non-Portuguese archives, as well as keeping northern Europeans out of South Atlantic ports.

Of the 27,233 voyages in the data set, 14,463 have no sources listed beyond that one initial source (termed SOURCEA in the data set). In fact, more than half of these apparently single-source records are taken from already published material where, in nearly all cases, additional primary references are to be found. Furthermore, other publications on which the present data set draws, such as Coughtry's listing of Rhode Island voyages, are based on a range of primary documents, but these are not listed by voyage in the publication itself. After allowing for these multi-source single references, it would appear that perhaps only one fifth of the 27,233 voyages are based on a single historical record, and the majority of these are for the Portuguese trade originating in Brazil. Well over half of the voyages in the set have three or more separate sources each, with the most abundantly referenced voyages, for the very large British trade between 1780 and 1807, averaging more than seven references per voyage. Researchers should no longer need to depend on data collected on the basis of a single source. The sources are listed in Appendix A.

While the sources are relatively rich, diversity brings a new set of problems. We can hardly expect that reports on voyages made several thousand miles—as well as several months—apart, often in different languages and under different bureaucracies, each with a separate set of official procedures to follow, would generate consistent information. For example, 137 voyages in the data set apparently arrived in the Americas with more slaves on board than when they left Africa. Others left port more than once on the same voyage, and some ships reportedly changed tonnage and even rig in the course of the voyage. The same ship occasionally appears under more than one name on the same voyage. Those used to working with a single source per voyage and generating data sets without any conflicting information should be warned that the editors have not attempted to correct all these problems. The data set offered here is by no means "clean" in the sense of being entirely internally consistent. We have pursued and eliminated many of the inconsistencies, but to eliminate all would have imposed an order on the historical record that anyone who has visited the archives (or indeed examined published sources such as Mettas or Richardson) knows does not exist. The editors always entered only one value per variable when faced with alternative information. In making such choices, we followed certain rules that researchers can change after going back to the sources. If users elect to do this, however, they, too, will have a set which is both not "clean" *and* not necessarily reflective of the historical records from which it is drawn.

New material tends to raise the question of the appropriateness of the variables used. The selection offered here has changed several times in the last six years and, given the fact that the set includes sources by voyage, will no doubt change again in the future as interests shift. The question of what ships to include is also to some extent arbitrary. The term "trans-Atlantic" is less straightforward than it appears. Omitting ships sailing to the Mascarene Islands was an easy decision, but several French ships in the late eighteenth century began their slaving activities in the Indian Ocean, but then on the same voyage brought slaves to the Americas after selling some Africans in Bourbon and the Cape of Good Hope. What to do with the British ships that carried hundreds of children from the Upper Guinea coast to Lisbon in the mid-eighteenth century? These we included on the basis of length of voyage. Should one include the Portuguese trade to São Tomé in the Bight of Biafra—probably the most enduring branch of the Atlantic slave trade? (Excluded on the same basis.) Then there were the more than 1,200 slave ships engaged in trans-Atlantic voyages, nearly half with slaves on board, that the British captured and carried into Sierra Leone, the Cape of Good Hope, St. Helena, Fernando Po, or Luanda, before they had been able to reach their intended American destinations. These we included. Or even more confusing, the 1,060 slaves awaiting shipment in barracoons in Ambriz, Angola, in May 1842, but carried off in British cruisers to St. Helena and Sierra Leone and never subjected to court proceedings of any kind, because they had never been on board a slave ship (excluded).[23] Limits had to be established arbitrarily, but at least the data set provides a basis for those who disagree with those limits to use our work to create their own data sets. Scholars also now have the opportunity to create subsets of slave voyage information beyond the 162 data variables provided here. The names of some slaves, names of Caribbean agents, names of crew, the details of shipboard insurrection, and much other information are not included in the present data set, but may be added fairly easily or linked with it via the unique voyage identification number.[24]

Each entry in our data set is a single voyage, assigned a unique identification number as the first of 226 pieces of information. These variables are of two broad types, *data* variables and *imputed* variables. The largest group, 162 in number, are *data* variables. They incorporate information collected from the sources. Users whose primary interest is in manipulating the data will no doubt download what interests them from among the data variables and consult the rest of the set sparingly. Other users, especially those who use only the CD-ROM interfaces, will find the second group of variables of greater interest. These 64 additional *imputed* variables form the basis of the tables, graphs and path graphics presentations that occupy most of the space on this CD-ROM. They are mainly imputed by us from our knowledge of the relevant voyage or adjacent voyages, or they are calculated directly from data encountered in archival or published sources.

DATA VARIABLES

The data variables include information that, for convenience, may be grouped into seven categories: (1) the vessel (name, tonnage, rig, guns, place and year of construction); (2) the shipowners; (3) the crew (captains' names, numbers of crew per voyage leg, mortality of crew per voyage leg, number of deserters); (4) the African captives (number, age, and gender of slaves purchased, embarked on the coast of Africa, disembarked in the Americas; mortality during the coastal trade, in the Middle Passage,

Table 1. Select Summary of Information Contained in the Trans-Atlantic Slave Voyage Data Set

Number of slave voyages in the dataset	27,233
Voyages with name of vessel	25,990
Voyages with name of captain(s)	22,115
Voyages with name of at least one shipowner	16,378
Size of crew provided on one or more voyage legs	11,265
Tonnage of ship available	16,406
Place of ship departure given	20,496
Date of ship departure given	19,261
Place(s) of embarkation on the African coast available	15,493
Numbers of Africans embarked reported	7,437
Voyages with age or gender of Africans reported	3,586
Place(s) of disembarkation available	20,403
Dates of arrival at place of disembarkation available	19,486
Numbers of Africans disembarked reported	15,778
Voyages reporting number of Africans died on board	5,130
Voyages with place of ship construction reported	8,635
Date of return to Europe or end of voyage given	10,100
Outcome of voyage indicated	24,646

Source for all tables: see the accompanying data set.

and in harbors in the Americas); (5) the areas of trade in Europe, Africa, and the Americas; (6) the dates of sail from each location; (7) the sources for each voyage. The codebook presents a complete listing of the 162 data variables in the data set. No voyage, however, includes information for all 162 fields. Table 1 provides a summary of the coverage for some of the more important data variables.

Generally, we attempted to preserve the written documentary record in adding to the data variables. Numeric variables, such as vessel tonnage, numbers of crew, and numbers of slaves, demanded a ranking of sources, particularly for the well-documented British trade. Regarding tonnage values, we preferred the Naval Office shipping lists (West India–based Colonial Office documents) over tonnages recorded in England—based on sources such as Admiralty records and *Lloyd's Registers of Shipping*.[25] As this implies, the British used several tonnage measurements before the late eighteenth century. The Registration Act of 1786 standardized these and, in general, raised tonnages for most British slavers that cleared customs after 1 August 1786, but there were at least two further changes in the first half of the nineteenth century.[26] Other nations had different tonnage measurements and thus comparisons of slave-per-ton ratios also should be treated with caution. Adjustments for these national differences and changes over time, as well as situations where the tonnage of the vessel was clearly overstated in response to government policy, are discussed at length below.[27]

Sources often report different numbers of slaves embarked on or "taken on board" the coast of Africa or landed in the Americas. Furthermore, for some years there are inconsistencies in slave age or gender totals per voyage. Regarding slave exports, we were careful to distinguish between the number of slaves purchased and the number who in fact were shipped from the coast.[28] We used slave export totals, whether reported by slave traders, African merchants, or European captains, agents, or merchants.[29] We included the slave export data reported in sources such as Gold Coast shipping departures, even though the totals often were rounded numbers, such as 400 or 500 slaves, and even though the totals occasionally were significantly less than the numbers of slaves who were disembarked in the Americas. Users should keep these biases in mind, not least for any calculations of mortality they may wish to try.

For slave import totals recorded in customs documents or shipping gazettes, we decided to use maximum totals, under the assumption that these differences might indicate deaths of slaves before slaves disembarked.[30] We preferred the sources that reported greater numbers of children on the voyage.[31] The Du Bois Institute data set includes variables for adult males ("men"), adult females ("women"), male children ("boys"), female children ("girls"), adults, children, and infants (reported often as "infants at the breast"). Unfortunately, age and sex definitions changed over time and among carriers. Arrivals in the early Iberian Americas were assigned a ratio of what a prime male slave would cost—the latter being termed a *pieça da Indes*. A child would receive a rating of half a *pieça*, a woman 0.8, and so on. In the early Iberian sources we have consulted the *pieça* and total numbers were reported in aggregate only, and it has not proved possible to infer age and gender breakdowns from aggregated *pieças*. In the 1660–1730 period, the London-based Royal African Company (RAC) defined children as about ten years of age or younger. For most of the British and French slave trades, a height (about four feet four inches) and/or age (about fourteen years) criterion distinguished adults from children. In the nineteenth century, captured slave ships of all nations, but mainly Spanish and Brazilian, had their human cargoes recorded by a variety of courts, some British, some international. There is little doubt that the criterion used to separate out adults was sexual maturity as assessed by physical appearance, which for most Africans at this time would probably occur in the mid-teens, but could vary according to the diet prevalent in the areas from which Africans were drawn as well as according to the eye of the beholders. Yet another categorization emerges from Cuban slave trade data (1790–1820) taken from the Seville archives, which adds "men-boys" and "women-girls" to the previous categories. These we included among men and women, respectively. All these measurements are of course imprecise, with even a clear age definition of "ten years and younger" hinging on casual inspection by Europeans, because many African cultures did not attach importance to knowledge of precise ages. In nineteenth-century court records, different officials often recorded slightly different distributions of the same group of slaves. However, the physiological correlation of height (specifically the teenage growth spurt) and sexual maturity means that there is broad similarity among most of these concepts, except for the RAC's definition, which excluded individuals that other definitions would have included as children. As the RAC records form the bulk of the age and gender information for 1660–1710, the share of children for this period is biased downward.

Dates of slave voyage sailings and arrivals are useful categories for sorting voyages in the data set. We therefore decided to broaden the definition of "departure" dates and we estimated years of arrival in the Americas for select voyages. For the non-British slave voyages, dates of departure generally refer to the date the vessels sailed from port. Sources do not always report precise dates of sail for the British trade. We assumed that the date crew entered pay (listed on Bristol or Liverpool muster rolls) was the date of departure (or close to it); and, for many voyages, this assumption is confirmed by analysis of other sources. Other "departure" dates included in the new slave trade data set are: the dates vessels cleared customs; the dates Mediterranean passes[32] were issued; the dates bonds were given; and the dates of vessel registration. These events usually occurred within a month of departure. London slave vessels cleared customs at Gravesend and often sailed from the "Downs," the shallows off the Kent coast. During contrary south-westerly winds, departures from the Downs were often delayed for several weeks. We included these dates of sail from the Downs as London "departure" dates. A separate variable defines these various "departure" dates. Reports of slave vessel arrivals in the Americas generally reached Europe within six to ten weeks. Without other documentary support we assumed the year or (in select cases) month of arrival, when the evidence was clear from the timing of gazette listings. Bristol and Liverpool muster rolls frequently record the dates the crew deserted ship or were discharged from pay in the Americas. For many voyages we assumed that these were arrival dates. When multiple dates were reported in the sources, the editors chose the latest dates for departures and the earliest dates for arrivals.[33]

For most voyage entries in the new data set, we maintained the spelling or wording of the names of vessels, captains, and merchants. Exceptions include corrections of obvious mistakes arising from the fact that the recorder of the information was often less than fluent in the language of the nation to which the vessel belonged. Even without this problem, variations of spelling were, of course, common before the nineteenth century and, as discussed below, we have standardized some spellings to facilitate sorting. We removed the article "the" from vessel names; thus we deleted *Le* or *La* from French names. Occasionally sources reported different names for the same vessel. The *Pretty Betty* is also identified, for example, as the *Pretty Peggy*. In such cases, we separated the two names with "(a)" to indicate an alternate name/spelling, as in *Pretty Betty* (a) *Pretty Peggy*. We attempted to maintain the consistency of captains' and owners' names throughout their voyage histories to facilitate the user's sorting of the file. Again, for some entries we placed alternate spellings after "(a)." We include three variables for captains in the data set. The ordering of these names indicates the order these men appeared, chronologically, in the documents. For some British and French voyages, sources list different captains during the ship's outfitting. A slave vessel may have cleared customs under the command of one captain but sailed to Africa under a subsequent captain. Evidence from the British trade suggests that for some voyages the first captain, rather than leaving the vessel, worked as a supercargo for the voyage. Therefore, we decided to keep the names and their ordering in the data set. The user will not be able to determine which captains were in charge of the vessels on the Middle Passage for all voyages. Some of the captains died before slaving on the coast; other captains' listings include the man who commanded the vessels on the homeward passages from the Americas. We kept all abbreviations in captains' names, consistent with the documentary evidence. From the Mettas-Daget catalog of French slave voyages, we attempted to maintain a consistent spelling of captains' names as indicated in the index to the two-volume French set. Double surnames and indicators of rank (*Sieur, Chevalier, de, de la*) pose problems singular to the organization of the French subset. In short, the spelling of names is not fixed in the French language. We followed the spellings preferred in the index, though we transcribed first-name abbreviations as indicated in the documentary evidence. To facilitate sorting the Du Bois Institute's file by captains' names, we maintained the ordering of surnames as indicated in the published index.

Similarly, we followed, as closely as possible, the spelling and ordering of shipowners' names given in the documentary evidence. The user will note some voyages "owned" by the RAC, Compagnie du Sénégal, or other monopoly trading groups. For these voyages, companies hired the vessels from shipowners and a group of partners or shareholders invested in the trading cargoes. The names of these individuals are not known. For most of the slave voyages in the Du Bois Institute data set, however, merchants owned fractional shares of the vessel and trading cargo. The listing of merchants in the set probably reflects the size of each shareholder, though this fact can be confirmed only for a few voyages.[34] For some voyages we only know the principal owner "and Company." This is true particularly for many Bristol (England) voyages. To indicate the fact that the voyage was owned and/or organized by additional owners, we placed an asterisk, *, at the end of the last recorded merchant's name, as in "Jones, Thomas*" (read: "Thomas Jones and Company"). For some other British voyages, father–son partnerships are listed, as in "Richard Farr, Sons and Company." For such voyages, we included the second owner with surname "Farr" as "Farr (Son)" and indicated that subsequent partners may be present by adding an asterisk after the third owner, "Farr (Son)*."[35]

Ownership information contained in the French slave trade documents presents additional problems for the researcher. Unlike the British trade, in which many records of extended partnerships survive, French documents usually list single *armateurs* who organized slave voyages. According to Stein, an *armateur* was "the merchant who organized and usually financed a large part of the slaving expedition."[36] Other merchant-investors, therefore, are not recorded in the documents. In cases in which additional owners are suggested by the words "company" (*Compagnie* or *Cie.*) or "associates" (*consorts*), we inserted an asterisk. Many French slave voyages were organized by family members. French documents include these familial relationships: brother(s) (*frères*), father (*père*), wife (*épouse*), widow (*veuve* or *vve*), eldest son (*fils* *aîné*), and son(s) (*fils*). These relationships are integral to the archival record and have been maintained in the Du Bois Institute data set. Because the French words *frères* and *fils* can imply multiple brothers and sons, we inserted an asterisk in the second ownership column, as in "Portier (Frères)*." In some cases, the document may record owners as "Brunaud Frères et Compagnie." For these few cases, we inserted a double asterisk as in "Brunaud (Frères)**." Some documents report the names of the *propriéteurs* who hired out their vessels to the *armateurs*, the *affreteurs* who freighted the slave ships, or the local agents who transacted business for absentee *armateurs*. We excluded these names from the Du Bois Institute data set. French owners' names often include complex double surnames and aristocratic titles. As in the case of French captains' names, we attempted to preserve the spelling in the original documents while following the Mettas-Daget index to standardize the basic spelling and name ordering.[37] We did this to allow the user to analyze ownership patterns easily through an A–Z owner–variable sort. The user should refer to the index of volume 2 of Mettas-Daget's *Répertoire* for a complete listing of the variant spellings of French merchants' names.

The new data set includes variables that report the place and year of construction for most vessels in the British slave trade. Merchants often purchased ships from other trades and converted them to slavers. The British slaving fleet also included prizes captured from the French, Spanish, Dutch, or Americans during the many wars of the eighteenth century. Shipping sources, such as *Lloyd's Registers of Shipping*, often do not distinguish whether a vessel was "French-built" or a "French prize." Similarly, the year of construction in the documents may refer to the year the vessel was captured or made free. As it is unlikely that many British merchants purchased vessels built in France in an open market, the user should assume that a "French-built" vessel was likely a war prize. Vessels reported as "French prizes," on the other hand, may not have been built in France. These ships could in fact have been built in Britain and subsequently captured and renamed by French merchants.

IMPUTED VARIABLES

The second group of variables comprises sixty-four items that are calculated or imputed from the data in the interest of making the latter more accessible or of compensating for missing information. To assist users who do not wish to perform a calculation every time they seek information from the data set, as well as to provide guidance for those who do, we have generated estimates that, in effect, fill some of the gaps in the existing variables. In addition, we have created some new series that are presented as new variables. Indeed, new variables were created whenever an imputed value was added to an existing variable. The imputed variables are derived directly from the data set, but are rarely compilations of raw data. The assumptions upon which these are based are explained more fully below, but mostly the derived variables are amalgamations or regroupings of the historical data from the first group of variables. To make the imputed variables as transparent as possible and to facilitate refinements, alternative assessments, and corrections that users might think necessary, we have included the SPSS program that creates the imputed variables on the CD-ROM.

The most straightforward of the imputed variables are geographic. The more than 600 locations in the data set where slave ships were built, registered, and cleared for a slaving voyage for disembarked slaves, are organized into just fifty-four places or regions shown in black letters on the accompanying maps. Departure points from Africa, also depicted in black letters, are grouped into eight regions. Each regrouping becomes a new variable. Because most slaving voyages lasted for many months or even years, users may choose from among three definitions of "year" for purposes of analysis: the year in which the voyage originated, the year of embarkation of slaves, or the year of arrival at point of disembarkation. When any one of these was unrecorded, an imputed value is derived from the next (or previous) stage of the voyage for which dates are available. We have assigned values for these three imputed variables to all records even though the voyage may have terminated prematurely. Years of arrival in the Americas are grouped into periods of five, twenty-five, and one hundred years. For the numbers of slaves carried and the numbers who perished during the voyage, as well as the age and gender categories, information is also frequently incomplete and additional imputed values are added, the creation of which is discussed more fully below. Researchers can of course make their own estimates and these, like the inferences on which alternative estimates are based, may well be different from what we regard as optimal. We would like to emphasize that in many cases the optimal is not obvious, and one researcher's estimates (and inferences) may be different from, but as good as, another's, despite the fact that all are working with the same data base. Anyone using the data, including ourselves, therefore needs to specify clearly the assumptions he or she is using.

The first problem is deciding whether a ship was a slave ship in the sense of intending to obtain slaves and carry them to another continent (the basic criterion for including a voyage in the data set). As late as the end of the seventeenth century, slaves formed less than half of trade by value between the Atlantic world and Africa. This implies that many ships went to Africa without trading for slaves. For most of the French and Dutch voyages to Africa, researchers other than ourselves have made the decision on whether or not a ship was a slaver, though we have uncovered a few additional voyages from these nations where the object of the voyage remains unclear. For many British and Portuguese voyages, however, we have had to make some hard decisions. Nearly five hundred British and North American voyages returned to the port of origin after an interval of time during which a slave voyage could have taken place, but no information survives of the places of trade in Africa or the Americas. For most of these ships, clearance was for "Africa and the Americas" and many of the remainder in this group are ships leaving British American ports for Africa. Before the nineteenth century, ships rarely went from the Americas to Africa for anything but slaves. In all these cases the ship is assumed to have been a slaver. For a further 1,500 voyages from Bahia in Brazil, even less is known. The main source of information on these is licenses of ship departures which specify "Elmina" (in West Africa) as the permitted destination. Large rolls of local tobacco were the trade good for African-bound Bahian ships, and in the eighteenth century slave traders of all nations depended on this tobacco. And as with North American Africa-bound ships, there is no evidence of a significant produce trade between Brazil and Africa. Gold was important in the first half of the eighteenth century and alcohol became more important later in the century, but return cargoes were always human. Late in the century about fifty of these voyages actually show up in British records from Cape Coast Castle, and in the nineteenth century there is very good overlap between these licences and the observations of British observers on the movements of slave ships. We have made the decision to include these Bahia–Africa voyages in the data set even though the additional information is not abundant.

There remains the question of produce ships—defined as ships that went to Africa for merchandise rather than people. In the British case we have evidence of nearly eight hundred voyages that went to the coast for produce, but not slaves, and, in addition, there were always a few "tenders" each year that went to the coast to get slaves for a larger ship, but did not themselves carry slaves across the Atlantic. Neither of these types of African voyages has been included in the set. For several hundred voyages, however, the information available is so scant that even the very basic question of voyage aim cannot be determined. In some cases, a ship left port with the intention of going to Africa, or even actually reached Africa, but its movements thereafter are not recorded. Records of ship departures have typically survived better in the historical record than records of ship arrivals. There are approximately fifty Dutch voyages that went to the coast in the early years of the Dutch free trade era in the 1730s that left no record beyond their departure. We have followed the decision of Johannes Postma in electing to keep these in the data set. Generally, for British "doubtfuls" we know only that the vessel took out a Mediterranean pass (a pass, in theory, protecting vessels from Barbary pirates) or cleared customs "for Africa."[38] We have excluded such voyages with the following exceptions: (1) vessels that we identified as trans-Atlantic slavers elsewhere in their voyage histories; (2) vessels to "Africa" commanded by slave-trade captains; or (3) vessels with particularly large crew-to-tonnage ratios, suggestive of vessels that required additional crew to control slaves.[39] As noted above, if the shipowner took out a pass for "Africa and the West Indies" or "Africa and America" we assumed that these vessels were slavers. For 379 other vessels, even this voyage-by-voyage assessment fails to clarify intent. We have elected to remove such voyages from the data set (they are therefore not included in the 27,233 total) and incorporated them into a separate file (included on the CD-ROM) complete with all the information we have uncovered. Researchers may choose to include these with the main data set, but all computations in the present publication are carried out without reference to them. These "doubtfuls" are troublesome, but their numbers, compared to the voyages about which we are quite certain, are not great.

Similarly, on the American side of the Atlantic, the editors often had to decide whether vessels carrying slaves were trans-Atlantic or inter-colonial slavers. For a few hundred ships arriving at ports in the Americas, doubts remain. Most of these voyages are to be found in Klein's set of voyages to Havana, 1790 to 1820, taken from the Spanish archives. It is clear that many smaller vessels were inter-island slave traders. That is, they trans-shipped African slaves from colonies such as St. Croix or St. Thomas, to Cuba. To separate the inter-island from trans-Atlantic vessels arriving in Havana with slaves, we used a benchmark total of 140 slaves—the average slave number on vessels in the sample that can be identified as trans-Atlantic slavers. Other researchers will use different ratios. Indeed, two members of the team that put together the set have already done so in earlier publications.[40] The Havana series does not report the African places of trade, and it follows that our omission of small trans-Atlantic slavers to Havana from the new slave trade data set does not make an impact on the sample size and analysis of the African origins of slaves disembarked in Cuba. Finally, not all voyages that crossed the Atlantic from Africa carried slaves. Generally we have assumed that all such voyages were slaving voyages, and have included them in the data set, though there is a slight possibility that a few of these vessels traded at nonslave markets on the coast. In summary, about 10 percent of the voyages included in the data set lack information about their activities after the voyages began. We nevertheless feel fairly confident that these were slaving voyages, and, as noted, those about which we feel less confident we have included in a separate file.

The first group of imputed variables, upon which the maps, analysis and summary screens draw, are geographical. Slave ships were constructed, were registered, set out from, and returned to different ports, as well as traversed the Atlantic twice in the course of a normal voyage. We have organized the points of construction and registration and places of departure and return given in the accompanying code book into fifty-four exclusive regions, all of which are depicted on the maps. These are grouped in turn into continent-wide categories. Alternatively, users may prefer to work with individual as opposed to regional or continental geographical locations. A full listing is contained in the code book, but space constraints prevent all these from being represented in the maps. We have adopted a convention that a place has to be mentioned ten times in the historical sources in order to win a listing in the maps, and this convention applies to points of embarkation and disembarkation of African slaves as well. Those wishing to use alternative groupings may use the code book supplied in Appendix C. For Europe and the Americas, the groupings are self-explanatory. For Africa eight regional definitions are employed. *Senegambia* is anywhere north of the Rio Nunez. *Sierra Leone* comprises the Rio Nunez to just west of Cape Mount inclusive. The *Windward Coast* is defined as Cape Mount up to and including the Assini River. The *Gold Coast* runs east of here up to and including the Volta River. The *Bight of Benin* covers the Rio Volta to Rio Nun, and the *Bight of Biafra*, east of the Nun to Cape Lopez inclusive. *West-central Africa* is defined as the rest of the western coast of the continent south of this point, and *South-east Africa* anywhere east of the Cape of Good Hope. A few locations, for example Casnasonis, Touau-Toro, and Cape Logas, cannot be identified, and one other major designation, a definition of the *Windward Coast* associated with no less than seventy voyages, straddles the definition of *Windward Coast* and *Sierra Leone* adopted here and is excluded from the African regional groupings.

Not all slave ships made it to the Americas, or even to Africa. Fortunately the data set is quite rich in information on the outcome of voyages. For almost 90 percent of the voyages we know if the ship obtained slaves, and for just over 90 percent we know if the ship reached Africa prior to initiating trade. Overall, almost one slave voyage in ten included in the present data set did not deliver slaves to the Americas, and only 82 percent of all ships reached the Americas under the control of the original owners. Some ships were captured by Africans or other Europeans, some were wrecked, others were destroyed as a result of resistance by the slaves themselves or captured by the mainly British cruisers that patrolled the Atlantic after 1807. A second set of assumptions that must precede any attempt to estimate trends from the current data thus relates to the fate of the ships and the slaves they carried.

The data set allows for 139 different voyage outcomes. As with the geographical variables, some regrouping is required to make these more manageable. The first regrouping (FATE2) takes the standpoint of the Africans on board, and asks where the ship disembarked its slaves. The majority were disembarked in the Americas, but about 13 percent in the present sample died during the voyage. In addition, some who left African ports actually disembarked in another part of Africa or on the island of St. Helena (about 5 percent in the sample). Most of this latter group were captured by British naval cruisers in the nineteenth century, though a very few, in the previous century, ended up in Europe.[41] A second regrouping (FATE3) is concerned with the fate of the ship and who might have interfered with its voyage. Slaves rebelled, shore-based Africans or pirates attacked ships, and one European power would often try to seize ships flying the flag of other powers, especially in wartime. Finally, a third regrouping (FATE4) takes the standpoint of the owners, and groups voyages on the basis of whether the ships reached the Americas, and if not, whether it was human agency or natural hazard that was responsible. As indicated, each of these three regroupings is represented by a different variable.

Establishing the outcome of the voyage is an important prerequisite to inferring information about both places of trade and numbers of people purchased. We have a good basis for imputing locations of slave trading as well as estimating the numbers of slaves embarked and disembarked. To return to the geography of the traffic first, for some voyages we know the intended ports of trade on the African coast and in the Americas. Private correspondence, newspaper reports, and official records of clearances from ports in Europe and the Americas frequently provide such information. Of the 27,233 voyages in the data set, at least 1,375 did not embark slaves, usually on account of capture or natural hazard. Of those that did, several hundred failed to complete the Middle Passage. The data set provides some information on African place of trade for 15,492 voyages or about 61 percent of those that are likely to have reached Africa. While this information surpasses current knowledge of the geography of the slave trade, it is possible to glean yet more. For 2,745 voyages that left Africa with slaves, or could have done so in the sense that the ship was not wrecked or captured prior to trade beginning, we may not know the African place of embarkation, but we do know where the captain *intended* to buy slaves. If we assume that he did in fact do so, then after eliminating those locations that are not easy to group into regions (for example the French designation *Côte d'Or*, which ranged from the Windward Coast to the Bight of Biafra), we are left with 17,551 voyages that contain useful information on place of African trade—or about 69 percent of those vessels in our sample that actually did or could have left Africa with slaves. Switching to the other side of the Atlantic, the data set yields some information on ports of arrival for 19,852 voyages, or 77 percent of those ships that disembarked slaves, or could have in the sense that there is no record of the loss or capture of the ship. Once more we have additional information on where 1,166 voyages *intended* to trade their slaves even though we cannot be certain that they actually did so. If we assume that captains completed the voyage according to plan, then the sample for places of disembarkation goes from 19,852 to 20,849 voyages (79 percent to 82 percent of those likely reaching the Americas)—again after eliminating place names of doubtful meaning such as "Caribbean," "West Indies," and "Brazil."

How valid are these assumptions? Most slave ships traded in the regions where owners declared they would trade. After eliminating captured ships that rarely completed their voyages as intended, as well as those ships with very broadly defined destinations ("Americas" or "British North America"), a sample of 888 voyages was derived with information on both intended and actual ports of arrival in the Americas. It was found that 82 percent of these vessels arrived at the ports for which they were bound at the outset of the voyages. A similar procedure for region of trade in Africa produced an equivalent figure of 72 percent trading at intended ports for 3,266 voyages that had information on both intended and actual regions of embarkation of slaves.[42] In addition, merchandise always had to be loaded in Europe and the Americas for a specific African region and was often impossible to sell in another region. It was unusual to find a specific manufactured good selling in more than one region.[43] Taken together, this evidence appears strong enough to allow us some modest inferences for those voyages that we know purchased slaves in Africa, or subsequently disembarked slaves in other parts of the Atlantic world, and for which the *intended* but not the actual region of trade is known. In the map display as well as the imputed variables, then, the intended region becomes the actual region for about 8 percent of the African regions and 2 percent of the regions of disembarkation.

In addition to these inferential issues, there is also some known bias in the data. The British signed three treaties with the Portuguese between 1811 and 1817 that contained clauses limiting Portuguese slave traders to regions of Africa south of the equator, and the last two of the treaties allowed British cruisers to capture Portuguese ships that did not adhere to these provisions. Brazil assumed these treaties when the country became independent in 1822. From 1815, slave ships arriving in Bahia, which had strong trading relations with the Bight of Benin or Slave Coast (north of the equator), usually reported their African port of departure as Cabinda or Malemba, ports just north of the Congo. British officials in Bahia, as well as naval officers patrolling the African coast, were convinced that all Bahian ships nevertheless continued to trade on the Slave Coast.[44]

A second set of inferences is suggested by the data on numbers of slaves leaving Africa and arriving in the New (and in some cases, the Old) World. Although 21,336 voyages in the data set arrived with slaves, and a further 4,347 could have done so, the sources provide the actual number on board at arrival for only 15,789 voyages. On the African side, the data are much weaker, with only 6,884 yielding information on the number of slaves leaving Africa, out of 23,040 voyages that left with slaves, and a further 2,788 that could have done so. Because most of those studying the slave trade are interested in the slaves rather than the ships, some inference would seem appropriate for those ships that traded without leaving anything in the historical record about the slaves they carried. The first step in making reasonable inferences is to draw on the numbers of slaves that might have been reported for the same voyage at an earlier or later stage of its itinerary.

Four hundred and eighty-two voyages left a record of the slaves they sold at various ports in the Americas, but not the numbers on board when they first arrived in the Americas. Unfortunately, slave sales at all ports were not always recorded, but for those that were, it is possible to add up the sales and impute the result as the total for slaves arriving.[45] Similarly, on the African side of the trade, 155 ships left a record of slaves carried from individual ports, but not of the numbers on board at the point of departure. Again a simple addition for those cases where the record of such individual ports seems complete provides an imputed total of slaves departed. A more aggressive procedure is adopted for a larger group of voyages that left information on the numbers of Africans taken on board prior to departure, but not the number disembarked at the end of the voyage, or vice-versa. Information on the numbers of slaves carried at some stage of the Middle Passage exists for a total of 17,592 slaving voyages (5,081 voyages have information on slaves carried at both arrival and departure, 1,803 for departures only, and 10,708 on arrivals only).[46] Imputed totals for the missing information may be made from a large sample of voyages that provide information on deaths during the passage.

The Du Bois Institute data set provides a good basis for estimating deaths during the Middle Passage. It contains 5,300 voyages with data on the number of Africans who died on board (for 5,104 of which a ratio of deaths to slaves embarked may be calculated). Of these, 4,672 made it to the Americas or sank while trying to do so (the remaining 432 voyages being mainly those of captured vessels that disembarked at Sierra Leone or other Old World ports). For reasons that are as yet poorly understood, deaths as a proportion of those embarked differed markedly by African region of embarkation. Tables 2 and 3 show breakdowns of shipboard mortality as a percentage of those slaves taken on board. Table 2 provides the descriptive statistics and Table 3 the results of a regression-based analysis of variance using Senegambia as the reference variable. The differentials between African regions are very marked; in fact, while the analysis is not shown here, after controlling for region of departure, they are greater than differences in (regional) mortality on ships arriving in the Americas. The breakdown of mortality ratios by African region is used here as the basis for imputing numbers arrived in the Americas where totals leaving Africa exist, and for numbers leaving Africa where the numbers on board at arrival in the Americas are known.

There remain 9,027 voyages with no information about how many slaves were on board. Indeed, for some of these we do not even know if they carried any slaves. This group breaks down into three categories. First are 5,483 cases that disembarked an unspecified number of slaves. Second are 756 ships that carried slaves from Africa, but then disappear from the historical record. Third are 2,788 ships that we can identify with some certainty as slave ships, but we do not know if they actually took on board slaves, much less disembarked them. For the first group, deriving an estimate of slaves carried involves separating out the small vessels that began their voyages in the Caribbean and mainland North America from those sailing from Europe and Brazil. Almost all slavers from the former areas obtained their slaves from Africa west of the Bight of Benin—Senegambia, Sierra Leone, the Windward Coast, or the Gold Coast. They disembarked on average 137.3 slaves, with no statistically significant difference

Table 2. Slaves Died on Board Ships Reaching the Americas as a Percentage of Those Embarked, by African Region of Embarkation, 1527–1866*

	Deaths/ Embarked (%)	Standard Deviation	Number of Voyages
Senegambia	11.9	12.7	279
Sierra Leone	11.0	15.5	157
Windward Coast	8.8	9.3	43
Gold Coast	11.4	13.1	617
Bight of Benin	14.7	14.8	631
Bight of Biafra	18.3	17.5	445
West-central Africa	8.4	10.5	1,865
South-east Africa	18.1	15.8	276
Nonidentifiable	16.7	16.6	332
All Africa	12.0	13.8	4,672

*Includes 196 voyages with zero deaths reported and excludes vessels disembarking in Africa.

Table 3. Regression-Based Analysis of Variance of Slaves Died on Ships Reaching the Americas as a Percentage of Those Embarked, by African Region of Embarkation, 1527–1866

Variable	Coefficient	Standard Error	t-score	Significance
Constant	0.119	0.008	15.2	0
Sierra Leone	−0.009	0.013	−0.67	0.493
Windward Coast	−0.033	0.018	−1.87	0.062
Gold Coast	−0.005	0.009	−0.55	0.582
Bight of Benin	0.028	0.009	2.92	0.003
Bight of Biafra	0.064	0.010	6.39	0
West-central Africa	−0.036	0.008	−4.25	0
South-east Africa	−0.064	0.011	5.58	0

among regions.[47] A figure of 137.3 is used as the estimate of slaves carried on voyages beginning in North America (including the Caribbean). Ships from Europe and Brazil, on the other hand, were likely to visit all areas of Africa where slaves were available, they were much larger, and they averaged 290.3 slaves disembarked with substantial variation among regions apparent.[48] For European and Brazilian voyages, the estimate takes into account these regional differences. Table 4 presents the average number of Africans disembarking from 9,376 of these ships. The imputed number of slaves disembarked from those ships where this information is missing is simply taken from this table, and the imputed number taken on board in Africa is the number disembarked with the addition of an allowance for mortality, as calculated from Table 2. For the 756 ships that carried slaves from Africa and then disappeared from the historical record, the assumption is made that all reached the Americas. The number of slaves at departure and arrival are estimated using the mortality loss ratios from Table 2 and imputed arrivals derived from Table 4.[49] Those voyages for which only a record of departure from the port of origin (or arrival in Africa) survives—ships that may or may not have carried slaves—are treated in a similar fashion. If the region, or intended region, of embarking slaves is known, then values in Tables 2 and 4 are used to derive imputed values for slaves arriving and departing. Finally, a separate allowance is made for those vessels arriving in the United States north of Maryland. On average, such vessels carried 73.8 slaves when leaving Africa and 64 on arrival in the northern states or colonies.[50] In summary, we have attempted to make allowances for missing numbers of slaves, but if a voyage disappeared from the historical record before disembarking or embarking slaves (because of natural hazard, say, or capture), it is assumed, for purposes of estimating the number of slaves carried, that the voyage was, in fact, successful from the viewpoint of the owner. As not all of these voyages could have been successful, there is some upward bias in aggregations of the volume of the slave trade that these estimated variables support.[51]

Table 4. Mean Number of Slaves per Voyage Disembarked in the Americas from Voyages Originating in Europe or Brazil, by African Region of Embarkation, 1527–1866

	Mean	Standard Deviation	Number of Voyages
Senegambia	164.5	101.1	514
Sierra Leone	217.4	116.1	498
Windward Coast	190.9	84.1	249
Gold Coast	277.4	120.3	1,062
Bight of Benin	326.2	144.0	954
Bight of Biafra	272.1	116.0	1,581
West-central Africa	338.9	141.3	1,836
South-east Africa	401.6	239.7	144
Unknown region	239.2	126.8	2,538
Total	273.4	139.0	9,376

The editors also used imputed values to account for the gaps in the data on slaves obtained at the various embarkation points on the African coast, before the ships began the Middle Passage, as well as missing data on slave arrivals at multiple ports in the Americas. In sending ships to the African coast, merchants selected cargoes for specific markets because Africans had regionally distinct preferences for the merchandise that they expected to receive in return for the slaves. Ninety-five percent of the cowries carried to the coast went to Bight of Benin ports. Almost all the metal shipped from Europe to Africa went to Senegambia or the Bight of Biafra, and manillas (wristlets) would sell only in the latter region. Almost all New England rum was sold on the Sierra Leone, Windward and Gold Coasts, and all roll tobacco from Bahia went to the Slave Coast. Textiles were welcomed in many places, but a pattern and texture that would sell in one place would often sell nowhere else. The point is that a ship leaving on a slave voyage would normally trade in only one region, though often at several ports in that region. It was unusual for ships trading in South-east Africa to buy slaves anywhere else, and the same is true for slavers trading in Angola, the Bight of Biafra, and, to a slightly lesser extent, Senegambia. A total of 15,493 voyages in the data set left a record of a place of trade in Africa. Only 1,785 of these, or 11.8 percent, traded at two or more places, and of these, only 812 voyages, or 5.4 percent of all voyages with information recorded on place of trade, traded at another place of trade *outside* the region in which the first trade occurred. Generally, then, if we know the region in which a ship traded, we can be reasonably certain that it did not trade in any other region, though it may have traded at more than one port. This is particularly the case if that region lay east of the Bight of Benin, the part of Africa, it might be noted, that supplied more than 60 percent of all the slaves entering the trade.

For those few ships that did trade in more than one region, nearly half (370) began buying slaves on the Senegambian, Sierra Leone, and Windward coasts before making the balance of their purchases—usually by far the larger share at that—at either the Gold Coast or the Bight of Benin. A further 151 voyages distributed their buying activities between the Gold Coast and Bight of Benin exclusively, and 139 traded on the adjacent Senegambian, Sierra Leone, and Windward coasts exclusively. There is thus a systematic pattern to the interregional trading activity on the African side that helps us to determine imputed numbers of slaves obtained from different regions when the hard data are missing. Ships trading down the coast before obtaining the bulk of their slaves at the Gold Coast had on average 21.8 percent of their final numbers on board when they arrived on the Gold Coast.[52] Those heading to the Bight of Benin had acquired just 14 percent of their slaves when they arrived there.[53] Slave ships trading only on the Gold Coast *and* the Bight of Benin had, on average, 25 percent of their final numbers on board when they arrived on the Slave Coast.[54] For ships trading in the three regions on the Upper Guinea Coast, as well as those involved in interregional trade elsewhere, the data are not sufficient to support estimates. The assumption is accordingly made that ships purchased equal portions of their final numbers of slaves in the different African regions in which they traded.

On the American side there were also broad systematic patterns of trading. Slavers in the large Brazilian trade typically sailed direct to the final ports, but farther north, the eastern Caribbean acted as a filter for all ships heading for the Caribbean and Central and North America. Many more ships called at Barbados, for example, than sold slaves in the island, as captains sought information on markets elsewhere in North America. If a ship called at a port but did not sell slaves there, we simply added the port to a count and reported the total as the number of ports of call prior to start of sales (NPPRIOR in the set). As noted above, disembarkation points exist for 20,403 voyages, but of these only 731 or 3.6 percent are known to have disembarked slaves at more than one port. To an even greater extent than on the African coast, ships sought out single markets, though it might be useful to remind readers that the data set makes no attempt to track slaves who were landed and then reshipped, however quickly, to other parts of the Americas (and Africa, for those who disembarked on the eastern side of the ocean). Asiento slaves destined for Spanish America and disembarked temporarily at Barbados, Curaçao, and Jamaica are thus counted as arrivals in these temporary staging areas. We divide voyages that disembarked at more than one location into two groups. Some ships made short trips to adjacent markets. Barbados and then one of the Leewards was one combination, Cap Français and Saint Marc another, Virginian ports and Maryland yet another. Others split their sales of slaves between the eastern and western Caribbean or the eastern Caribbean and North American mainland markets. For analytical purposes, regions of first disembarkation were grouped into the western Caribbean (defined as west of Hispaniola) and mainland North America together on the one hand, and the eastern Caribbean on the other. This regrouping may be found in variable

REGDIS11. Second or later regions of disembarkation were grouped into minor markets (the northern colonies), the Lesser Antilles and Maryland, and the Greater Antilles together with the major mainland markets such as Virginia, the Spanish Americas, and the Guianas. These subsequent disembarkation points are regrouped into variable REGDIS21. As might be expected, vessels trading first in a major western Caribbean or mainland Americas market before moving on to another similar market distributed their slaves fairly equally between the two trading regions.[55] Ships disembarking first in the smaller markets in the eastern Caribbean sold varying ratios of the total on board depending on where the subsequent market might lie. Those heading for similar eastern Caribbean markets (for example landing slaves at one Leeward island before proceeding to another) left behind 44 percent before proceeding to the next market, while those sailing to the major markets on the North and South American mainlands or the Greater Antilles left a much smaller share of their original manifests at their first markets—27 percent.[56] These percentages are used to estimate numbers of slaves left at these markets by ships with no data on slaves. Where voyages disembarked at three different ports—a pattern exhibited by less than 1 percent of the ships in the data set—then the proportion going on to later ports is assumed to be split equally between second and third ports.

The above procedures generate estimated figures, where necessary, for the data used to produce series of slave departures and arrivals for eight different regions in Africa and fifty-four different islands/regions in the Americas. Total slave arrivals are the sum of slaves disembarked. The point to note here is that partial cargoes and full cargoes are in four different variables, one containing the total arrived or departed and the other three reflecting purchases (or sales) in possibly three different places. Any series of departures or arrivals requires a search of all four, and selecting the region in the query screen will generate such a search and computation. No estimates are provided here for individual ports, as opposed to regions. Users could employ the above procedures to obtain these fairly easily, however.

As already noted, the demographic structure of the trade—the age and gender composition of the Africans carried off as slaves—is well represented in the data grouping of variables. Some modest inferences, however, are required to present an accurate picture of any age and gender pattern that requires computations of two or more voyages. Ships left the African coast with widely differing numbers of people on board. It makes little sense to combine, say, the *Merced,* taken into Sierra Leone with only one man slave on board, and the *Alerta,* which landed 69 men among 606 slaves disembarked in Havana in September 1818. The ratio of men in the first voyage was 100 percent, the ratio in the second case was 11 percent. Averaging without any further adjustment produces a ratio of men of 56 percent, which, given the different numbers of people on board, misrepresents historical reality. With large numbers of cases, this problem will tend to be unimportant, but if users select a small number of cases, they should employ a simple weighting technique to correct for the differences in the number of people being counted. Thus, in the above example, the weighted average of men on the two ships is very much closer to the 11 percent on the *Alerta* than the 100 percent on the *Merced*. Alternatively, users might disregard our voyage-based age and gender ratios and simply divide the total of males (or females) by the total number of slaves in the sample they select.

Users should also note that age and sex information was recorded on some vessels at the beginning of the voyage and others at the end of the voyage. We have created composite male and child ratio variables that lump together information from both ends depending on availability, and where information has survived on both we gave precedence to the ratios at the point of disembarkation. This procedure was justified by the fact that shipboard mortality was only modestly age and sex specific, and those users who wish to elimate these modest effects should use the MALRAT1, MALRAT3, CHILRAT1 and CHILRAT3 variables instead of the imputed variables, MALRAT7 and CHILRAT7.

We have also made some assumptions in order to project a fuller picture of national carriers in the trade. The set identifies the national affiliations of 23,302 or 86 percent of the voyages in the data set. For a further 2,462, the context of the voyage and the name of the shipowner or captain make inferences about place of registration possible, and thus we created an imputed variable of national affiliation that contains affiliations for 25,764 voyages. For some ships, this step is not possible. From 1839, the British allowed their cruisers to take slave ships flying the Portuguese flag into British Vice Admiralty Courts for confiscation under British law. In response to this (and to similar legislation in 1845 that extended the provision to the Brazilian flag), many slave ships abandoned ship registration papers altogether. In addition, there are undoubtedly some voyages that registered in one country but that belonged to nationals of another, and others that sailed under false papers. Some British ships sailing under the French flag in the late eighteenth century are examples of the first; both British and United States owners sailing with Portuguese and Spanish papers after 1807—sometimes fraudulent, sometimes not—are examples of the second. Overall, these cases probably account for less than 1 percent of the ships included in the data set. It is also difficult to separate voyages made by ships owned in Britain from those owned in the British Americas and later the United States. Some ships identified as "British" were likely registered in the British Americas, and a similar problem arises with the Portuguese and Brazilian ships in the nineteenth century. A frequency count of this new variable is nevertheless of interest and indicates that 11,166 voyages were British with a further 1,791 registered in the British Americas. Of the other principal nations, 5,152 are identified as Portuguese, with a further 1,034 as Brazilian; 4,031 were French; 1,238 were Dutch; 1,107 were Spanish; and 200 were likely Danish, although some of these could have been made by Brandenburg ships. Many of the voyages of unknown nationality were likely Portuguese, but even if they all were, this distribution would still illustrate the point made earlier about Portuguese voyages being underrepresented in the set.

The final imputed variable discussed here is tonnage. This is probably the least reliable of all the estimated variable provided in the Du Bois Institute data set. It is offered here as a guide to ship size and to provide a crude basis for calculating indices of crowding on ships for both slaves and crew, as well as a basis for examining the efficiency with which the trade was conducted over time and between major ports and carriers. The reasons for the relative unreliability of this variable begin with the differences between deadweight tonnage, tons burden (for loose-packed cargo), and freight tons (for merchandise). But even within these types, jurisdictions often had their own methods of computation.[57] Sometimes more than one method was used simultaneously, and in most countries the various methods changed over time. In England, for example, the RAC, the Naval Office shipping returns, the Royal Navy, and *Lloyd's Registers of Shipping* all appear to have computed tons differently until 1786, when the measured ton became standard by Parliamentary statute. The formula was changed in 1836. It is possible to ignore some of these (the Royal Navy, which did occasionally carry slaves to the Americas, appears to have used the same formula as the RAC) and develop an equivalency for some others. But some jurisdictions introduced political bias because tonnage might be tied to subsidies or figures might be altered to circumvent the efforts of another branch of officialdom to control the numbers of slaves carried per ton.

The standard adopted here is the one established by the largest of national traders when the slave trade was at its height. Beginning in 1773, British ships were required to use measured tons as well as registered tons in their official documentation; from 1786, measured tons alone became the standard.[58] After 1807, slave ships were not usually of British origin, but reports of their activities originated from or were transmitted through British channels. Much of the data were converted into British tons in the process. Reports from the British Vice Admiralty Courts almost invariably list British tonnage, and in 1840 the Foreign Office instructed its overseas "observers" to give tonnages as provided in the ships' papers where possible, as well as in British tons.[59] Many tonnage data, however, are from non-British jurisdictions. Several independent contemporary observers suggested that the Portuguese (and Brazilian) ton was perhaps 5 percent smaller than its 1773–1835 British counterpart, and the Spanish ton 50 percent larger.[60] The differences between Portuguese and British tonnage for the nineteenth century, at least, seem small enough to disregard. A regression equation is estimated for converting Spanish into British tons that suggests that the former was perhaps two-thirds larger, with the difference varying somewhat by size of ship.[61] United States tonnages are taken to be the so-called "Custom House Measure" of 1789, which was modeled on the British formula. Although some differences existed in the application of this rule among American ports, no adjustment is made here.[62]

For the period before 1786, a further regression equation is estimated for converting RAC tonnages into the pre-1786 registered ton.[63] Also for this period, the Dutch ton, or *last*, is taken to be double the size of the British registered ton, and the French *tonneau de mer* is treated as equivalent to the British registered ton.[64] In addition to these adjustments, it is, of course, necessary to convert all pre-1786 tonnages to the standard British measured ton adopted for the set. Once more the British registered-to-measured conversion formulae are called into service. There remain several tonnages for British ships between 1714 and 1786, the provenance of which we are not certain. We have used registered tons wherever we could, but much of the data were collected by others and it is not always clear which tonnage measurement is used.[65] We have made the assumption that such tonnages were the same as registered tons down to 1786. As noted above, ships could use either the registered or the new measured ton in their papers between 1773 and 1786, but slavers sailing before and after 1773 appear not to have changed their tonnage. Finally, it should be noted that there are almost no Spanish and Portuguese tonnage observations in the set before 1773 and very few Dutch tonnage records after 1786. No conversion has been attempted for Scandinavian, Hanseatic League (or Brandenburg), Sardinian, or Mexican tonnages, values for which thus do not appear in the TONMOD variable.

One last tonnage adjustment (not made here) is required for known bias. Tonnages of French slave ships between 1784 and 1792 were inflated (that is to say the size of the ton was deflated) substantially, as the French government based their subsidy of the slave trade on tonnages.[66] The size of the bias is unknown and tonnages of French ships in this period are simply ignored in the conversion procedure. A second bias (also not made here) is apparent in Portuguese tonnages between 1815 and 1830. A Portuguese law of 1684, and clauses in the 1815 and 1817 Anglo-Portuguese slave trade treaties, limited Portuguese and later Brazilian ships to a ratio of between 2.5 and 3.5 slaves per ton, depending on the construction of the ship.[67] Ratios were normally lower than this in every branch of the trade for which data survive, and the regulation must have had little practical impact. As pressure to suppress the trade mounted in the nineteenth century and conditions on board deteriorated, it is possible that these strictures began to have some application. In any event, British officials in Brazil between 1815 and 1830 (after which the complete Brazilian trade was illegal and such regulations became moot) became convinced that the Portuguese tonnage measurements were being inflated by 60 percent on average so that more slaves could be confined on board.[68] The issue cannot be resolved on the available evidence and no adjustment is made here, but users have been warned.

INTERPRETATIVE WORK

The work of interpreting the data offered in this CD-ROM is just beginning. Nevertheless, it may be useful to draw the attention of users of the data to some of the issues that scholars have been exploring through use of material contained in the Du Bois Institute data set. Many of these issues have been raised by the project's principal researchers. The conclusions reached in discussing some issues are preliminary in nature, because the work was presented while the data set was still being compiled and was necessarily less complete than the final version in this CD-ROM. The following is intended, therefore, to give an indication of some of the issues that the data set has been used to explore, and of possible lines of further inquiry, rather than as a package of solid conclusions.

Material from our data set has, to date, been largely disseminated through conference presentations.[69] Papers drawing on the data set have been given by Eltis, Richardson, and Behrendt at the Collegium for African American Research (CAAR) conference at Tenerife in February 1995; by Eltis and Richardson, by Behrendt, and by Engerman and Klein at the Social Science History Association conference at Chicago in November 1995; by Behrendt at the Social Science History Association conference at New Orleans in October 1996; by Behrendt and Eltis at the annual American Historical Association conference at New York in January 1997; by Richardson at a conference on the Impact of the Transatlantic Slave Trade on the Cultures of the Americas, held at Kingston, Jamaica, in February 1997; and by Behrendt, Eltis, and Richardson at a Summer Institute on Identifying Enslaved Africans: The "Nigerian Hinterland" and the Creation of the African Diaspora, held at York University, Toronto, in July 1997. The issues raised by these various papers have principally been concerned with long-term geographical patterns of slave shipments from Africa and arrivals in the Americas and linkages between the two continents; the human costs of slaving as measured by the mortality of slaves and of crews of slave ships; and the cultural repercussions for the Americas of the forced migration of Africans. Revised versions of some of the papers presented at these meetings have been published, notably in a volume edited by Eltis and Richardson.[70] This last collection also includes a brief introduction to the new slave trade data set. Some of the other papers presented at conferences will be published soon. In addition, several other papers that draw on evidence included in the Du Bois Institute data set have been published. Among these are papers by Eltis and Engerman on the age and gender structure of slave shipments; by Eltis and Richardson on long-term productivity trends in the slave trade; by Eltis on the volume and African coastal distribution of British and other slave shipments, 1662–1714; and by Behrendt on the British slave trade, 1780–1807.

For Europe and the Atlantic Americas, one of the major patterns to emerge from the data is the pervasiveness of the slave trade. All the Atlantic ports in Western Europe and the Americas as well as a host of minor shipbuilding centers were heavily involved in the business at one point or another. Within these ports, ownership was widely based. The old picture of a small dominant elite organizing and benefiting from the traffic is in need of revision. Particularly in England, slave ships would have four or more owners, ownership concentration ratios were very low, and small investors were numerous. The ownership base appears to have been wider in England than in France, and captains were more likely to have an ownership share in a venture in both England and in the United States than in continental Europe.[71] As might be expected from an activity with strong European connections, the data provide an excellent perspective for assessing long-run economic and business trends within Europe. Despite—indeed, because of—the fact that the commodities traded were human, it is possible to track long-run productivity trends in this trade more easily than in any other business. Small secular improvements may be discerned, but there were also differences in productivity among the major national carriers, and, indeed, among ports within national areas. Analyses of tonnages, crew, slaves carried, and voyage lengths indicate that British preeminence in the eighteenth century trade was rooted in an efficiency advantage.[72] Specifically, the British carried more slaves per crew member and per ton, and their voyages were faster than those of other Western European slave traders. The data set should open up new opportunities for scholars to evaluate the impact of the slave trade on Europe as well as on Africa and the black Americas.

The other side of productivity trends, of course, is the conditions under which people—both crew and slaves—traveled, as well as the contentious issue of how many traveled. The set establishes with more clarity than ever before that slaves and crews were far worse off than their counterparts on board ships in the contemporary trans-Atlantic indentured servant traffic and on convict ships heading to both the Americas and Australia, as well as on galleys operating in Mediterranean and Atlantic coastal waters. On the issue of the mortality of slaves and crews on board ship, it is now possible to get a more definitive picture. The business was deadly for both slaves and crew—though the basis of the mortality and morbidity of the two groups was different. Mortality rates (taking into account time at risk) were more severe for slaves, and crew and slave mortality rates differed by African region of trade. These systematic variations are not easy to explain on the basis of influences controlled by Europeans alone.[73]

The impetus for much modern research on the slave trade stemmed, as noted earlier, from Curtin's census of the Atlantic slave trade, published in 1969. The issue of the volume of the trade remains very much alive (it should be obvious that while the present data set is large, it does not claim to be a population in the statistical sense). Almost without exception, reappraisals of Curtin's findings have tended to suggest that he underestimated the scale of slave shipments from Africa to the Americas. This consensus has recently been broken by Behrendt, who finds that, as far as the British slave trade in 1780–1807 is concerned, Curtin overstated slave shipments from Africa.[74] Although confined to the British trade, Behrendt's findings are nevertheless significant. The volume of the British slave trade in the quarter century before its abolition in 1807 has been the source of much controversy. Moreover, it is important to note that Behrendt lowered all previous estimates of the volume of the British slave trade from 1780 onward not because of a lowered estimate of the number of ships leaving Britain for Africa—a central issue in earlier debates on the scale of British slave trafficking in this period—but because of an increased estimate of ships lost before they embarked slaves on the African coast. The literature has neglected the latter issue, yet, as Behrendt's work shows, such losses could be substantial, especially in wartime when privateering activity was widespread. As war was a frequent event in Western Europe in the century and a half after 1660, its impact on the outcome of slaving voyages needs to be taken more fully into account in estimating the volume of the slave trade. The Du Bois Institute data set is particularly strong on the fate of voyages, drawing on sources in several countries. It also provides hitherto inaccessible detail on individual ports at all phases of a trans-Atlantic slaving venture. The consolidated set will be vital to future assessments of the volume of the slave trade for periods outside 1780–1807 as well as for particular branches of the trade.

These new data are obviously useful in dealing with European issues and the quantitative issues of volume, mortality, and productivity. It is probably not too early to point to two even more important, though still emerging, applications of the data. The first is the issue of African agency in the Atlantic world, put firmly in the center of the late twentieth-century Atlantic history research agenda by John Thornton's recent work.[75] The second and related general issue is the nature of trans-Atlantic connections. Europe and the Americas have long dominated studies of trans-Atlantic exchanges, but now Africa should be given a larger role.

The issue of African agency is basic to much of the work made possible by the data set. The coastal distribution of slaving activity in Africa, for example, has attracted much recent attention because it relates, inter alia, to some central questions for historians, notably the impact of the slave trade on Africa as well as its legacy for the cultural history of the Atlantic world. As with the question of the trade's volume, Curtin's census provided the initial benchmark study of regional patterns of slave shipments from Africa in 1700–1867. The picture described by Curtin was amended in the two decades after 1969 by others using sources of shipping data unavailable to Curtin, and further refinements to it have recently been proposed by the compilers of the Du Bois Institute data set.[76] The latter have suggested that West Africa's share of slaves shipped to the Americas was rather larger than previously assumed, accounting for perhaps 48 percent of the total in 1595–1867. Moreover, among the West Africa provenance zones, the Gold Coast and Bight of Benin seem to have been more important than was earlier thought. While the Du Bois Institute data set has helped to redraw regional patterns of slave shipments from Africa, perhaps its main contribution to discussion of the origins of slaves lies in its disaggregation of regional patterns and its identification of specific ports of call of ships on the coast. This represents a major advance, enabling scholars to begin to reconstruct histories of slave shipments from subregions or even single ports in Africa. Preliminary analysis by Eltis and Richardson has suggested that there was a high level of concentration of slave shipments through a small group of ports in Africa, with trade in most regions being heavily centered at no more than two or three principal outlets.[77] Tracing changes in the relative contribution of ports to slave shipments from regions may, in turn, shed light on the changing dynamics of slave supply in Africa. As our knowledge of trading patterns within regions deepens, so will our appreciation of regional and local variations in conditions surrounding the conduct of the slave trade within

Africa. In this respect, the Du Bois Institute data set offers new insights into African influences on the structure of the trans-Atlantic slave trade.

Other studies deriving from the Du Bois Institute data set provide additional reminders of the impact of regional or local conditions in Africa on the conduct and outcome of slaving voyages. Thus, for example, shipboard slave mortality is relevant not just for understanding the human experience of crossing the Atlantic and variations in European attitudes toward peoples different from themselves, but also for understanding local conditions in Africa, including, in part, the enslavement process. We now know that slave mortality in the Atlantic crossing tended to decline after 1700, largely as a result of technical, institutional, and organizational changes. Significant differences in trans-Atlantic mortality levels by region of embarkation of slaves in Africa remained after allowing for these long-run trends and persisted throughout the history of the traffic in slaves, a finding confirmed by the sample of voyage data that underpin Table 2 in this introduction. According to Klein and Engerman, these regionally related differentials in oceanic mortality highlight the need for closer study of enslavement processes in Africa and of the march by slaves to the sea.[78]

Further differences in patterns of slaving in Africa have been revealed by studies of the composition of slave shipments, of shipping productivity, and of slave insurrections. Thus, Eltis and Engerman have shown that there were observable and continuing variations in the gender structure of slaves shipped by African region between 1663 and 1864, with, for example, proportionately more females being included in shipments from the Bight of Biafra than from other regions.[79] The proportions of males and children among shiploads of slaves carried from all the major slave supply regions in Africa increased during the final two centuries of the trans-Atlantic traffic. As one might anticipate, the scale of the change varied somewhat between regions, but in each region the rise in proportions of children entering the trade was steep, notably in the nineteenth century. As Eltis and Engerman have observed, a number of "major economic and social issues related to Africa and the Americas are at stake" when one begins to explore the causes of these shifts in the composition of the slave trade.[80] These include the role of female labor in agriculture in Africa, American planters' preferences for male labor, and the demographic histories of societies on the two sides of the Atlantic. Africa is at least as important as the Americas to explaining these patterns. Similarly, Eltis and Richardson have demonstrated that, while there were long-run swings in the productivity of shipping in the slave trade, there were also sizable variations in loading times of ships—as well as in the mean number of slaves carried per vessel—among African regions.[81] Finally, a recent preliminary, and, as yet, unpublished analysis of shipboard slave revolts and attacks on ships from the shore has suggested that there were some remarkable regionally related differences in the incidence of violent endings of slaving voyages.[82] Specifically, the costs of doing business were greater in some areas than others because of the nature of African resistance. Explanations for these differences in regional characteristics still have to be uncovered, but their existence underlines the variability of trading conditions encountered by European and American traders in precolonial Africa. The differences remind us once more not only of the value of both regional and comparative approaches to the study of slaving in Africa and its implications for the continent, but, more important, of the larger question of African agency. The vast majority of Africans involved in the slave trade may not have been willing participants, but it is now time to recognize that their ability to shape the trade whether slaves or slave traders was no less than that of the Europeans.

But perhaps the major findings yielded by the data relate to trans-Atlantic connections.[83] To date, studies of such linkages have assumed a highly aggregative approach, but uncovering microlinkages is possible and will be an important feature of future research. The Du Bois Institute data set makes available unprecedented detail on which parts of Africa supplied the different parts of the slaveholding Americas, and we expect that this new information will have an important influence on the debate on the impact of African heritage on New World societies. The distribution of Africans in the New World was no more randomized than it was for Europeans. Even with their limitations, the maps of trans-Atlantic movements of African slaves that have been drawn are instructive. Broadly, with the exception of the Reconçavo of Bahia, and probably the province of Minas Gerais for which Bahia was a conduit, the African role in the repeopling of South and Central America was as dominated by West-central Africa as the European role was by Iberians. Peoples from the Congo basin and Angola formed by far the greater share of arrivals in South-central Brazil—the largest single slave reception area in the Americas—as well as in Northeastern Brazil, Central America, and, to a lesser extent, Rio de la Plata. West-central Africa formed the second largest provenance zone for all other South American regions. Bahia—one of the two most important points of entrance into the New World for Africans—was a major exception. In Bahia, the dominance of peoples from the hinterland of the Bight of Benin was almost complete. A large West African presence was also apparent in Spanish mainland America and the less important region of Rio de la Plata. The latter, in fact, was the only region on the continent of South America where Africans from the Bight of Biafra—overwhelmingly Igbo and Ibibio peoples—were to be found in large numbers. West Africa was also well represented in the Guianas and Surinam; but as in Central America, it was the Gold Coast, rather than the Bight of Biafra and the Slave Coast, which supplied almost half of those arriving. This was the only region in the whole of South America where peoples from the Gold Coast had a major presence.

In the Caribbean, West Africa was as dominant as was West-central Africa in South America, though generally the mix of African peoples was much greater here than it was further south. Only in St. Domingue did Africa south of the equator provide half of all arrivals. And only in the French Leewards and Cuba did that ratio approximate one third. Generally, a single West African region was a clear leader in supplying each specific American region. Barbados, the Danish islands, and Spanish Central America—utilizing mainly the Dutch entrepot of Curaçao—drew disproportionately on the Gold Coast. The Bight of Benin played a similar role for the French Leewards. In Jamaica and the British Leewards, the Bight of Biafra was easily the single most important provenance zone, though in none of these cases did a single region, unlike the situation in all Brazilian regions, provide as many as half of all arrivals. In the Caribbean, "West Africa" effectively meant the Gold Coast, the Slave Coast (Bight of Benin), and the Bight of Biafra. Senegambia was of some importance in the French Caribbean, and the long Windward Coast stretching south from Sierra Leone was responsible for almost a fifth of disembarkations in the British Leewards; but generally, these regions played a minor role in the slave trade to the major American regions. The relative proximity of Senegambia and the Windward Coast to the Americas—passages from Senegambia to the Caribbean were typically half as long as more southerly trans-Atlantic crossings—suggests some factor other than geography was at work.

Of all the receiving areas in the Americas, Cuba and Barbados received the greatest mix of African peoples, although the United States was not far from this pattern. No single part of Africa supplied more than 28 percent of arrivals in either island and the only major regions not well represented were South-east Africa in Barbados and the Gold Coast in Cuba. In addition, the region that supplied the greatest number of slaves—West-central Africa—covered a wider range of coastline by the nineteenth century and drew on a vast slaving hinterland, suggesting a further mixing of peoples. Moreover, there was no regional segregation within Cuba. Almost all the arrivals moved through Havana and ports in the west of the island and, for the rest of their lives, worked in the sugar and coffee plantations that formed the hinterland of these ports. Large numbers of Yao from South-east Africa, Yoruba from West Africa, and Lunda from the Kasai Valley in the Angolan interior intermingled in the plantation labor forces. They arrived, moreover, within a relatively short space of time in the first half of the nineteenth century, a pattern that clearly separates Cuba from Barbados and the United States. Cuba, then, was an exception. An examination of shifts over time in these trans-Atlantic links suggests that some American regions, such as Bahia and South-central Brazil, drew on the same part of Africa throughout the slave trade era; other American regions, such as the British and French areas, may have drawn on a mix of African provenance zones, but tended to do so in sequence—a sequence that, in the British case, was played out very slowly. Perhaps the picture of a confusing mix of African cultures with all the attendant barriers to establishing African influence on the New World needs revising.

Geography and Atlantic patterns of winds and ocean currents help to explain some of these trans-Atlantic linkages, particularly within the so-called South Atlantic System. But other patterns, including the Bight of Benin–Bahia and the Bight of Biafra–West Indies connections, are less easily explained by reference to geography or transport economics. European influences were also important. With the exception of the Spanish colonies, the great majority of the slaves arriving in the Americas did so in ships belonging to subjects of the colonial powers governing the territories in question. It follows, therefore, that linkages between African and

American regions reflected in part the patterns of influence by national groups of carriers over trade in specific African regions or ports.[84] But it is the African role that requires more attention. Why should Europeans as a group focus first on the Bights and later on West-central Africa, when regions in Upper Guinea were both closer to the Americas and provided larger ratios of the males that we are told planters in the Americas wanted? Why should loading (or slaving) times on the African coast lengthen well before the peak period of departures and then fall in the last quarter of the eighteenth century when the trans-Atlantic slave trade was at its height? Why should some African peoples (for example, the Yoruba) have left more easily identifiable legacies in the Americas than others (for example the Igbo), even when the latter outnumbered the former among forced migrants? It is not likely that answers to these and many other key questions will come from the European side of the slave trade. Of more immediate importance, such questions could not even be framed without these new data.

As the above implies, the new information on trans-Atlantic links bears heavily on the issue of the cultural implications of the slave trade, especially when taken in conjunction with the findings on the demographic structure of the slave trade. Traditionally, culture is an area of study not much affected by quantitative findings. Generally, more adults and more females traveled across the Atlantic in the seventeenth and early eighteenth centuries than later in the trade. While long-distance migrations are typically dominated by young adult males, it may well be that the larger the female component—especially females of childbearing age—the greater is the impact of the migration on both areas of departure and areas of arrival. Cultural and language transfers are likely to be greater where more opportunities for family formation exist among the migrant group. Generally, a much larger proportion of those leaving West Africa were likely to be women than were those leaving either Upper Guinea or West-central Africa (Upper Guinea combines the Senegambia, Sierra Leone, and Windward Coast regions used in Tables 2–4). In addition, West-central Africa was always likely to have much greater proportions of children entering the trans-Atlantic trade than were other provenance zones. More dramatically yet, the proportion of children entering the trans-Atlantic trade more than tripled between the seventeenth and nineteenth centuries, while the share of women fell by well over 50 percent in the same period. Thus, to the extent that cultural transfers between Africa and the Americas occurred, they were likely to be stronger in the earlier period in those regions of the Americas, specifically British America, that drew on West Africa. The degree to which enslaved Africans drew on or adapted their own heritage in seeking to rebuild their lives in the Americas has become a major issue among scholars. The patterns of trans-Atlantic flows of African slaves revealed by the Du Bois Institute data set promise to add further impetus to scholarly debate and offer opportunities for exciting new interpretations. This point is reinforced by the fact that new information on various aspects of the slave trade, including catchment zones in Africa, slave ethnicity, and inter-colonial movements of slaves, may be linked to the present data set.

Overall, perhaps the single most important preliminary feature to emerge from these new data is the large role of Africans in the Atlantic world. Decisions on who entered the trade, where slaves embarked and disembarked, and where the trade first began and first ended emerged from an exchange between Africans—both elite, and, via resistance, enslaved—and Europeans. We hope that the data will contribute to the recent trend in the study of Africa and Africans that sees Africans as more than just victims. We also hope the data will allow a much clearer view of trans-Atlantic connections between Africa and the Americas and promote a fresh evaluation of the role of the slave trade in European and African societies, value systems, and economic development.

NOTES

1. For the modern equipment used by slave traders in the last phase of the slave trade, see Great Britain, Public Record Office, Foreign Office Slave Trade series 84 (henceforth FO84), Admiralty to Lord Russell, 19 August 1864, enc., piece 1229.
2. Regarding cycles of slave exports see Stephen D. Behrendt, "The Annual Volume and Regional Distribution of the British Slave Trade, 1780–1807," *Journal of African History*, 38 (1997), 187–211.
3. Philip D. Morgan, "The Cultural Implications of the Atlantic Slave Trade: African Regional Origins, American Destinations and New World Developments," in David Eltis and David Richardson (eds.), *Routes to Slavery: Direction, Ethnicity and Mortality in the Atlantic Slave Trade* (London, 1997), 122–42.
4. On the general issue of African influence on the Americas see John K. Thornton, *Africa and Africans in the Making of the Atlantic World, 1500–1680* (Cambridge, 1992). On the specific trans-Atlantic connections between the rice-growing Gambia River area and the disproportionate number of "Gambia" slaves purchased by Carolina rice-growing planters, see Daniel Littlefield, *Rice and Slaves: Ethnicity and the Slave Trade to Colonial South Carolina* (Urbana, 1981).
5. Herbert S. Klein, unpublished data sets, *English slave trade, 1791–1799 (House of Lords survey); Slave trade to Havana, Cuba, 1790–1820; Slave trade to Rio de Janeiro, 1795–1811; Virginia slave trade in the eighteenth century, 1727–1769; Slave trade to Rio de Janeiro, 1825–1830;* and *Angola slave trade in the eighteenth century, 1723–1771* (University of Wisconsin–Madison Data and Program Library Service, 1978). Much of the interest in this work was, of course, generated by the publication of Philip D. Curtin, *The Atlantic Slave Trade: A Census* (Madison, 1969).
6. Jean Mettas, *Répertoire des expéditions négrières françaises au XVIIIe siècle*, Serge and Michèle Daget (eds.), 2 vols. (Paris, 1978, 1984) (cited hereafter as Mettas-Daget, *Répertoire*); Serge Daget, *Répertoire des expéditions négrières françaises à la traite illégale (1814–1850)* (Nantes, 1988); David Richardson (ed.), *Bristol, Africa, and the Eighteenth-Century Slave Trade to America*, 4 vols. (Bristol, 1986–1996). In addition Eltis had created a data set of 5,378 slave voyages, 1811–66, for his study of the nineteenth-century Atlantic slave trade (David Eltis, *Economic Growth and the Ending of the Transatlantic Slave Trade* (New York, 1987), 399–404), which was unpublished but was available in machine-readable form.
7. The principal source for this file was the Liverpool Plantation Registers, 1744–1786, to which was added information from *Lloyd's Lists*, Liverpool newspapers, customs accounts,

and Naval Office shipping lists. This was published subsequently as David Richardson, Kathy Beedham, and Maurice M. Schofield (eds.), *Computerised Edition of the Liverpool Plantation Registers, 1744–1786* (ESRC Data Archives, University of Essex, 1992).

8. Postma compiled records of 1,211 Dutch slave voyages, 1675–1802, for his study of the Dutch slave trade (Johannes Menne Postma, *The Dutch in the Atlantic Slave Trade, 1600–1815* (New York, 1990), 305–7); and Stephen D. Behrendt organized a file of 2,990 British slave voyages for his study of the last decades of the British trade ("The British Slave Trade, 1785–1807: Volume, Profitability, and Mortality." Ph.D. thesis, University of Wisconsin–Madison, 1993).

9. Jay Coughtry, *The Notorious Triangle: Rhode Island and the African Slave Trade, 1700–1807* (Philadelphia, 1981), yielded a list of 927 Rhode Island slave voyages; 650 voyages to the Spanish Americas appeared in Elena F. S. de Studer, *La Trata de Negros en el Rio de la Plata duranta el Siglo XVIII* (Montevideo, 1984) and Colin Palmer, *Human Cargoes: The British Slave Trade to Spanish America, 1700–1739* (Urbana, 1981); 571 Portuguese slave voyages to the Spanish Americas were extracted from Enriqueta Vila Vilar, *Hispano-America y El Comercio de Esclavos: Los Asientos Portugueses* (Seville, 1977). To these should be added 169 Danish slave voyages, 1698–1789, in Svend E. Green-Pedersen, "The Scope and Structure of the Danish Negro Slave Trade," *Scandinavian Economic History Review*, 19 (1971), 149–97, and Waldemar Westergaard, *The Danish West Indies under Company Rule* (New York, 1917).

10. We are grateful for unpublished slave voyage information provided by Svend E. Holsoe (slave trade to Danish colonies), Joseph E. Inikori (British slave trade, 1764–88), Jim McMillin (slave trade to the United States, 1783–1807), Joseph C. Miller (slave trade to Brazil, 1811–19), James A. Rawley (mainly London voyages, 1715–79), Robert L. Stein (French slave trade), and Wim Klooster (Dutch slave trade).

11. Thus Shawn Miller was able to work with the Arquivo Publico documents that Pierre Verger had used in *Flux et Reflux de la Traite de Nègres entre le golfe de Benin et Bahia de Todos os Santos* (Paris, 1968), translated as Pierre Verger, *Trade Relations Between the Bight of Benin and Bahia, 17th to 19th Century*, trans. Evelyn Crawford (Ibadan, 1976).

12. In the grant application in 1992, 21,000 voyages was stated as a possible total for the set. In 1994, we thought 24,000 possible (Stephen D. Behrendt and David Eltis, "Research Note on the Atlantic Slave Trade Database Project," *Newsletter of the Institute of Early American History & Culture* (Summer 1994), 2). In fact the published set contains 27,233 voyages and further additions are possible. Almost all the additional voyages are from primary sources. The new sources consulted include: *Lloyd's Lists*, 1702–4, 1741–1808; PRO, Liverpool port books, 1698–1726; Mediterranean Passes for London, 1730s–1770s; and Barbados Treasurers' Accounts, 1740s–1770s; Arquivo Publico da Bahia, Passaportes de Embarcações, Series 439, 440, 443, 447, 449, 456, and Biblioteca Nacional do Rio de Janeiro, *Documentos Históricos da Biblioteca Nacional do Rio de Janeiro*, 110 vols. (Rio de Janeiro, 1929–55), vols. 61, 62.

13. For additional information on the creation of the Du Bois Institute data set, see David Eltis and David Richardson, "The 'Numbers Game' and Routes to Slavery," in Eltis and Richardson (eds.), *Routes to Slavery*, 2–5.

14. These results confirm a recent assessment of the completeness of the Mettas-Daget catalog. See David Eltis, "The Volume, Age/Sex Ratios and African Impact of the Slave Trade: Some Refinements of Paul Lovejoy's Review of the Literature," *Journal of African History*, 31 (1990), 550–67.

15. Thus, for example, the burst of activity from French ports between August 1678 and May 1679 in the aftermath of French conquests of Dutch factories in the Senegal region is underrepresented in the set. Abdoulaye Ly (*La Compagnie du Sénégal* (Paris, 1993), 152–4) lists 21 ships going to Senegal, and concludes that 16 of these were slave ships (8 bringing slaves to

France and 8 to the French West Indies), but it is possible to identify only 7 of these as slave ships.

16. Paul Lovejoy, "The Volume of the Atlantic Slave Trade: A Synthesis," *Journal of African History*, 23 (1982), 473–501, and idem, "The Impact of the Atlantic Slave Trade on Africa: A Review of the Literature," *Ibid*, 30 (1989), 365–94.

17. Lovejoy estimated 367,000 slaves left Africa between 1450 and 1600 ("Volume of the Atlantic Slave Trade," 477–8).

18. Respectively, $n = 6,771$, $sd = 177.4$; $n = 14,769$, $sd = 158.6$.

19. The sample of voyages with information on slave numbers at the point of departure is rather smaller than the sample of those with known numbers on board at arrival. There is some indication that a disproportionate number of the former sample were drawn from the Upper Guinea region where ships and numbers embarked were smaller than elsewhere on the African coast.

20. Joseph Inikori has recently given "a preferred global figure of 15.4 million for the European slave trade." Adjusting for those carried to the offshore islands and Europe, this implies 14.9 million headed for the Americas. See *Cahiers d'Etudes africaines*, 32 (1993):686.

21. See David Richardson's entry in Seymour Drescher and Stanley L. Engerman (eds), *A Historical Guide to World Slavery* (Oxford, 1998). It should be stressed that this estimate was made quite independently of the Du Bois Institute data set.

22. H.C.V. Leibbrandt, *Precis of the Archives of the Cape of Good Hope*, Vol. 14, *Journal 1662–1670* (Cape Town, 1901), 127–8.

23. British slave ships trading from Africa to Lisbon include the *Kent* (1731), the *Mary* (1737) and the *Betsey and Hennie* (1755). For sources see the data set. For the removal of slaves from Ambriz to St. Helena and Sierra Leone, see Kelly Muspratt to Aberdeen, 31 July 1843, FO84/501.

24. Behrendt linked a subset of Liverpool voyages to the core set for his study on crew mortality (Stephen D. Behrendt, "Crew Mortality in the Transatlantic Slave Trade in the Eighteenth Century," in Eltis and Richardson (eds.), *Routes to Slavery*, 60).

25. For an example of variant tonnage values for British slave vessels, see David Richardson and M. M. Schofield, "Whitehaven and the Eighteenth-Century British Slave Trade," *Transactions of the Cumberland and Westmorland Antiquarian and Archeological Society*, 92 (1992), 197–8.

26. For a discussion of early English tonnage rules see David D. Moore, *Site Report: Historical & Archaeological Investigations of the Shipwreck "Henrietta Marie"* (Key West, Fla., 1997). One of the imputed variables taken up below (TONMOD) contains our attempt to adjust tonnages to reflect the new measurement for ships which did not undergo any structural changes, as reported in *Lloyd's Registers of Shipping*, 1782–1788. In looking at slave "crowding" on British slavers in the eighteenth century, users of the data set should keep in mind the fact that tonnages—for the same size vessels—are comparatively greater after 1786, and the variable TONMOD is a more reliable indicator of trends in ship size over time than are the unadjusted tonnage data.

27. Robert Louis Stein, *The French Slave Trade in the Eighteenth Century: An Old Regime Business* (Madison, 1979), 41; Patrick Villiers, "The slave and colonial trade in France just before the Revolution," in Barbara Solow (ed.), *Slavery and the Rise of the Atlantic System* (Cambridge, 1991), 228.

28. Captains often trans-shipped slaves among vessels before sailing from the coast.

29. Old Calabar merchant Antera Duke reports the number of slaves embarked on twenty-four British merchant slave vessels, 1785–7—without naming the ships. We have been able to identify all of these (Daryll Forde (ed.), *Efik Traders of Old Calabar. Containing the Diary of Antera Duke, an Efik Slave-Trading Chief of the Eighteenth Century* (London, 1956), 40–5). In presenting evidence before Parliament in 1788–99, British captains and merchants fre-

quently mentioned numbers of slaves shipped from the coast. The numbers of slaves who were embarked on the coast are reported most fully in the French sources.

30. See Behrendt, "British Slave Trade, 1785–1807," 57–8.

31. One frequently cited shipping list reports that there were no children on board several British slave voyages in the 1790s (House of Lords Record Office, House of Lords, Main Papers, 28 July 1800). This document, however, omitted to report the children embarked (cf. PRO, T70/1574; House of Lords Record Office, House of Lords, Main Papers, 14, 25 June 1799).

32. In theory, these documents allowed British vessels to pass freely through the "Mediterranean" waters frequented by Barbary corsairs. The pass records vessel and captain's names, tonnage, the date the pass was issued, and intended trading location, such as "Africa" or "Africa and the Americas" or "Barbary" or "Madeira." See David Richardson, *The Mediterranean Passes* (Wakefield, 1981).

33. For example, when British slave vessels arrived in the West Indies, the date the vessel cleared customs (an arrival date reported in some sources) was sometimes 2–4 weeks earlier than the date the surgeon deposited his medical log (an arrival date reported in other sources).

34. A few fractional shares of Liverpool slave voyages, for example, are known from 1786 to 1788. See Robert Craig and Rupert Jarvis (eds.), *Liverpool Registry of Merchant Ships* (Manchester, 1967). We do not have variables in the Du Bois Institute data set which record these fractional shares.

35. Similarly, for the Dutch firm Jan Swart & Zoon (son), we entered the second owner as "Swart (Zoon)."

36. Stein, *French Slave Trade*, xv. Some *armateurs* also may have owned the vessel. French dictionaries define *armateurs* firstly as those merchants who fit out the ship or expedition and secondly as (ship)owners (E. Littré, *Dictionnaire de la Langue Française* (Paris, 1881), I, 194).

37. The *armateur* "Deridelière Le Roux" organized fifteen Nantes slave voyages, 1754–76. There are eleven alternative spellings of this name, including "Des Ridelières le Roux" and "Leroux Derridelière" (Mettas-Daget, *Répertoire*, II, 874, 880).

38. *Lloyd's Lists* indicates that some of these "African" destinations included the Iberian Peninsula, Northern Africa, or the southern African whale fishery.

39. A complete examination of the Seaman's Sixpence ledgers, held at the Public Record Office (ADM68 series), would confirm that some of these "Africa"-bound vessels were trans-Atlantic slavers. The Sixpence ledgers record Caribbean locations of trade; slave vessels often can be identified quickly by large crew-per-ton ratios.

40. Herbert S. Klein, *The Middle Passage: Comparative Studies in the Atlantic Slave Trade* (Princeton, 1978), 220–1, used 200 slaves on board to distinguish ships arriving from Africa from those trading slaves within the Caribbean. David Richardson, "Slave Exports from West and West-Central Africa, 1700–1810: New Estimates of Volume and Distribution," *Journal of African History*, 30 (1989), 8n, assumed that ships arriving with more than 75 slaves on board were trans-Atlantic vessels.

41. The relatively high proportion of slaves in this category is a reflection of the recent and good-quality British government records that exist for this diverted branch of the forced migration. In reality, over the whole period of the trade less than 2 percent of all slaves would find themselves remaining in the Old World, and even some who did were soon transported to the Americas under an indentured labor rather than a slave regime.

42. For a previous use of this procedure see Behrendt, "British Slave Trade," 196–7. Variables compared were REGARRP and MAJSELRG for the Americas and EMBREG and REGEM1 for Africa.

43. One of the most widely used contemporary surveys of African regional preferences was Lt. Edward Bold, *The Merchants and Mariners' African Guide* (London, 1819). For a very de-

tailed private record see the manuscript in the Sidney Jones Library, University of Liverpool, "Memorandum of African Trade, 1830–1840," for W.A. Maxwell and Co.

44. See Verger, *Trade Relations*, 358–61, and David Eltis, "The Export of Slaves from Africa, 1820–43," *Journal of Economic History*, 37 (1977), 417–20, for a fuller discussion.

45. Excluded from this procedure were eighty voyages which reported sales of less than one hundred at only one port (mainly at Barbados, frequently the first port of call in the Americas).

46. Note that this breakdown includes voyages with information of slaves on board at *any* phase of the voyage (partial purchases and sales as well as mortality on board, all of which were sometimes reported without any information on totals of slaves departed or arrived). The numbers are thus somewhat greater than those reported in rows 10 and 14 of Table 1.

47. $N = 809$, $sd = 119.5$.

48. $N = 14,318$, $sd = 155.7$.

49. Actually, of slaves on board at arrival minus imputed deaths from Table 2.

50. $N = 24$, $sd = 31.6$; and $N = 17$, $sd = 37$, respectively.

51. Further refinements are possible, but not attempted here. For example, users may wish to separate periods of peace from periods of war in making future estimates.

52. $N = 49$, $sd = 21.7$. It should be noted that this is actually the ratio on board when the ship arrived at its principal market for slaves on the Gold Coast. In several cases the ship may have traded at other Gold Coast ports before reaching this point. This ratio therefore is biased upward, with the true proportion of slaves obtained at non-Gold Coast ports lying below this figure.

53. $N = 17$, $sd = 13.6$. It should be noted that this is actually the ratio on board when the ship arrived at its principal market for slaves in the Bight of Benin. In several cases the ship may have traded at other Bight of Benin ports before reaching this point. This ratio therefore is biased upward, with the true proportion of slaves obtained at non-Bight of Benin ports lying below this figure.

54. $N = 27$, $sd = 22.3$.

55. Mean numbers disembarked in the first region were 43.5 percent of all slaves disembarked. $N = 38$, $sd = 31.0$.

56. Respectively, $n = 60$, $sd = 32.4$; and $n = 169$, $sd = 25.8$.

57. For discussion of the general problem see Frederick C. Lane, "Tonnages, Medieval and Modern," *Economic History Review*, 17 (1964–5), 213–33.

58. The 1773 legislation is 13 Geo III, c. 74. See W. Salisbury, "Early Tonnage Measurements in England: I, H.M. Customs and Statutory Rules," *Mariner's Mirror*, 52 (1966), 329–40. To convert registered tons into measured tons, we used the formulae in Christopher J. French, "Eighteenth Century Shipping Tonnage Measurements," *Journal of Economic History*, 33 (1973), 434–43. The 1786 act is 26 Geo III, c. 60, and its 1835 counterpart is 5 and 6 Will IV, c. 56, which introduced different rules for empty ships (s. 2) and those with cargo (s. 6). As the latter appears to have been used on slave ships, it is the one adopted here, and a further regression equation allows us to convert post-1836 tonnages into the measured ton of 1773–1835. It is:
$$Y = 52.86 + (1.22 \times X) \quad N = 63, R^2 = 0.77$$
where Y = measured tons, 1773–1835, and X = measured tons after 1835.

59. Palmerston to Kennedy, May 4, 1840 (circular dispatch), FO84/312.

60. H. Chamberlain to Canning, 18 Sept. 1824 (enc.), FO84/31; W. Cole and H. W. Macaulay to Palmerston, 1 Jan. 1835 (enc.), FO84/169; W. W. Lewis and R. Docherty to Palmerston, 9 Sept. 1837 (enc.), FO84/214; J. Barrow to Aberdeen, 16 May 1842 (enc.), FO84/439; G. Jackson and F. Grigg to Aberdeen, 2 Jan. 1841 (enc.), FO84/350.

61. Unfortunately, we do not have sufficient pairings to warrant a more refined analysis. The equation is:
$$Y = 71 + (0.86 \times X) \quad N = 32, R^2 = 0.66.$$
Where Y = British measured tons, 1773–1835, and X = Spanish tons.

62. *Statutes at Large*, Vol. 1, p. 55. For a discussion see W. Salisbury, "Early Tonnage Measurements in England: IV, Rules Used by Shipwrights and Merchants," *Mariner's Mirror*, 53 (1967), 260–64.

63. See David Eltis and David Richardson, "Productivity in the Transatlantic Slave Trade," *Explorations in Economic History*, 32 (1995), 481, for the formula.

64. See Lane, "Tonnages, Medieval and Modern," 217–33 for a discussion.

65. James A. Rawley, for example relied heavily on the tonnages in *Lloyd's Register of Shipping* in the data on London ships which he supplied to us. It is not clear how this publication derived its tonnage measurements.

66. Stein, *French Slave Trade*, 40–1; Villiers, "The slave and colonial trade in France," 228.

67. See Klein, *Middle Passage*, 29–31.

68. See for example H. Chamberlain to Canning, 7 July 1824 (enc.), FO84/31.

69. A complete list of the papers mentioned in this paragraph may be found in Appendix B.

70. Eltis and Richardson (eds.), *Routes to Slavery:*

71. David Eltis, David Richardson, and Stephen D. Behrendt, "The Structure of the Transatlantic Slave Trade, 1595–1867," paper presented to the Social Science History Meetings, Chicago, 1995; Rachel Chernos, "The Atlantic Slave Traders and their Communities in the Eighteenth and Nineteenth Centuries." M. A. thesis, Queen's University, 1997.

72. Eltis and Richardson, "Productivity in the Transatlantic Slave Trade," 420–42.

73. Behrendt, "Crew Mortality in the Transatlantic Slave Trade," and Herbert S. Klein and Stanley L. Engerman, "Long-Term Trends in African Mortality in the Transatlantic Slave Trade," both in Eltis and Richardson (eds.), *Routes to Slavery*, 36–71.

74. Behrendt, "Annual Volume and Regional Distribution," 187–211.

75. Thornton, *Africa and Africans*.

76. David Eltis and David Richardson, "West Africa and the Transatlantic Slave Trade: New Evidence of Long-Run Trends," in Eltis and Richardson (eds.), *Routes to Slavery*, 17.

77. *Ibid*, 22–9.

78. Klein and Engerman, "Long-Term Trends in African Mortality in the Transatlantic Slave Trade," in Eltis and Richardson (eds.), *Routes to Slavery*, 46.

79. David Eltis and Stanley L. Engerman, "Fluctuations in Age and Sex Ratios in the Transatlantic Slave Trade, 1663–1864," *Economic History Review*, 46 (1993), 310–11.

80. *Ibid*, 309.

81. Eltis and Richardson, "Productivity," 478.

82. David Eltis, Stephen D. Behrendt, and David Richardson, "Cooperation and Resistance: African Shaping of the Transatlantic Slave Trade," unpublished paper presented at the Institute of Commonwealth Studies, London, May 1997; Stephen D. Behrendt, David Eltis, and David Richardson, "The Bights in Comparative Perspective: the Economics of Long-Term Trends in Population Displacement from West and West-Central Africa to the Americas before 1850," unpublished paper presented at the Summer Institute on the African Diaspora from the "Nigerian" Hinterland, York University, Toronto, July 1997.

83. Much of the following two paragraphs is based on Eltis, Richardson, and Behrendt, "Structure of the Transatlantic Slave Trade, 1595–1867"; Eltis and Richardson, "West Africa and the Transatlantic Slave Trade," 16–35; and Morgan, "Cultural Implications of the Atlantic Slave Trade," 122–45, all in Eltis and Richardson (eds.), *Routes to Slavery*.

84. Stephen D. Behrendt and David Eltis, "Competition, Market Power, and the Impact of Abolition on the Transatlantic Slave Trade: Connections between Africa and the Americas," unpublished paper presented at the American Historical Association, annual conference, New York, 1997.

APPENDIX A: LIST OF SOURCES

The sources listed here are not exhaustive. Previously published compilations of data on the slave trade that have been incorporated into the present data set list the sources on which they have drawn in their own bibliographies. The present list includes references to these published data sets only, and not to the sources which they use unless we have consulted the latter. In several cases we have returned to the primary material, in which case the primary reference is included here, but not the secondary source. It follows that some well-known secondary sources are omitted from the present bibliography.

For twenty-seven voyages, all from the nineteenth century, the source has been misplaced. The voyage information has been left in the set and these records may be readily identified by the blank in the source A variable.

The source variables in the data set have only limited space available, and the information they provide is, of necessity, brief. The bibliography provides the full reference, and abbreviations in brackets to the right of the full references below represent the citation or part citation in the source variables of the data set itself. If no abbreviation is provided, then the first few letters or numbers in the full bibliographic reference correspond to the abbreviated information provided in the source variables.

Primary sources are organized by location, secondary sources by author.

DOCUMENTARY SOURCES

1. BRAZIL

Bahia

Arquivo Publico   [APB]
Passaportes de Embarcaçoês, Series 439, 440, 443, 447, 449, 456

2. DENMARK
Holsoe archive; Danish Customs and Harbor Master Records   [holsoe]

3. GREAT BRITAIN

Bristol
Society of Merchant Venturers, Merchants' Hall,   [SMV]
Muster Rolls, Wharfage Books

Cumbria
Pooley Bridge, Dalemain House   [Hasell]
Hasell Family Papers

Edinburgh
Scottish Record Office,   [Seaforth]
Seaforth Papers

Greenwich

National Maritime Museum   [NMM]
Ship's logs: Log/M/21; AML/V/13

Hull

University of Hull
Notes of Maurice M. Schofield on Liverpool slave ships between 1774 and 1778 held
   at the School of Economic Studies.   [Schofield archive]
   Wilberforce Papers

Keele, Staffordshire

University of Keele, Archives
Raymond Richards Collection, Davies-Davenport Papers   [DTA]

Liverpool

Liverpool Museum mss,
Accounts of "Calveley" and "Eadith," 53–34
Papers of John Knight, 71–190–2

Liverpool Record Office
Case and Southworth Papers, 380 MD 33–36   [C&S]
Holt and Gregson Papers, 942 HOL, volume 10   [LivRO]
Leyland papers 387 MD 40-44   [Leyland]
Roscoe Papers; Letters of William Roscoe, 920 ROS   [Roscoe]
Slavery & Privateers, No. 5   [Slavery&Privateers]

National Maritime Museum on Merseyside, Albert Dock, Liverpool
Earle Family Papers   [Earle]

University of Liverpool Library
Dumbell papers 10/46–52   [Dumbell]

London

Bank of England
Papers of Humphry Morice, B43–51   [BankEng]

British Library   [Add.Mss]
Additional Manuscripts
3984, Sloan manuscripts
19560, Le Sieur des Marchais, "Journal de Navigation du Voyage de la Coste de
Guinée..." from January, 1704 to January, 1706
25495–8, 25500–5, 25556, 25562, 25567, South Sea Company, Papers, Minutes and
Correspondence
38416, Jenkinson, Charles (1st Earl of Liverpool), Official and Private
Correspondence
39946, "Narrative of Voyages to the Guinea Coast and the West Indies, 1714–1716"
43123, 43125, Aberdeen Papers

House of Lords Record Office

Main Papers, House of Lords, 1794–1800 (Dates supplied in data set)   [HLRO,MP]

Public Record Office (**Class, piece number**)

Admiralty Records
Adm6/207
Adm7/77, 78, 80, 82–4, 86–92, 94, 96, 98, 100, 102, 136, 373, 375, 630
   (Mediterranean Passes and Impress Protection)
Adm68/194
Adm123/173, 174, 179

Audit Office
AO16/1, 4–5

Board of Trade
BT6/3, 31, 127, 188
BT98/33–8, 40–69
BT107/8–10

Chancery
C103/130, 132–3 (Papers of Thomas Hall)
C107/1–15 (Papers of James Rogers)
C108/212, 214 (Papers of John Leigh)
C109/401 (Papers of Samuel Sandys)
C111/95 (Papers of Thomas Hall)
C113/262, 272, 276–89 (Papers of William Petrie)
C114/1–3, 154–8 (Papers of Thomas Lumley)

Colonial Office (includes Naval Office Shipping Lists)
CO1/18, 19, 31, 34, 44
CO5/508–11, 710, 749, 1441–50
CO10/2
CO27/12, 27
CO28/11, 20, 25, 29–34
CO33/12–23, 30
CO76/4–7
CO103/130
CO106/1–4
CO137/88
CO140/89
CO142/13–25
CO152/7, 10, 15, 16, 19, 21, 22, 32, 33, 37
CO157/1
CO228/34
CO243/1
CO267/1

CO268/1
CO278/7
CO290/1–2
CO300/16
CO308/1
CO317/1
CO388/10, 11, 13, 25
CO390/7

Exchequer
E190/1374/7 to 1406/3 (King's Rembrancer [Port Books], Liverpool)
    E219/340 and 377

Foreign Office
FO63/168, 169, 192, 194, 202, 230
FO83/2349
FO84/3 to 1267
FO308/1,2

High Court of Admiralty
HCA37/1–3, 5–6
HCA42/2
HCA49/97, 101
HCA97/49

Privy Council
PC1/3678, 3696, 3714, 3720, 3734, 3738, 3740, 3743, 3764

State Papers
SP 29/47

Treasury
T64/48, 286
T70/1–3, 5, 7–18, 20, 23, 26, 28, 50, 51, 56–58, 61, 62, 66, 76, 158, 167–70, 175,
    176, 309, 350, 355,376, 584, 599, 600, 646, 869, 885, 909, 913–25, 933, 936–60,
    962–69, 972–3, 1209, 1209B, 1213, 1222, 1225, 1263, 1438, 1463, 1472, 1476,
    1484, 1498, 1515, 1517–19, 1522–32, 1534–38, 1544–59, 1561–74, 1577–87,
    1699 (African Companies' Papers)

University of London
Brougham manuscripts   [BroughamMss]
Simon Taylor Archive (Institute of Commonwealth Studies)   [ST]
I: C,D,E,F,G; XIII: A; XIV: A

Manchester

John Rylands University Library Archives   [JRL]
English mss, MS 517 3(a)

Oxford

Bodleian Library
Rawlinson mss., C745–747 (See also, Robin Law, below)   [Rawl]

Rhodes House Library
Anti-Slavery Papers, British Empire Manuscripts, s.22, folders G77–80   [B.E.mss]
Buxton manuscripts (Papers of Sir Thomas Fowell Buxton), British Empire Mss.,
    s.444, volumes 17, 23–4, 26–34, 38–46   [BxMss]

4. PORTUGAL

Lisbon

Arquivo Historico Ultramarino
Bahia, Angola   [AHU]

5. UNITED STATES

Ann Arbor, Michigan

University of Michigan, Clements Library
Anti-Slavery Collection, I   [CL]
Shelburne manuscripts, volumes 43, 44

Columbia, South Carolina

South Carolina Department of Archives and History
Duty Books of the Public Treasurer of South Carolina, Journals A-C, 1735–76
                                                                         [SC,Treasury]

Hamilton, New York

Hamilton College, Beinecke Library
West Indies Collection, Book 569   [Beinecke]

Madison, Wisconsin

University of Wisconsin Library
Data sets of slave trading voyages collected by Herbert S. Klein and deposited at the
    University of Wisconsin archives, Madison, Wisconsin. These sets are described in
    Klein, *The Middle Passage: Comparative Studies in the Atlantic Slave Trade*
    (Princeton, 1978). They are held at Wisconsin as follows:
  Klein, Rio de Janeiro data-set,1795–1811
  Klein, Rio de Janeiro data-set,1825–1830
  Klein, Angola data-set,1723–1771
  Klein, Havana data-set,1790–1820
  Klein, English Slave Trade, 1791–99
  Klein, Virginia Slave Trade in the Eighteenth Century

New York

New York Historical Society
Slavery Collection, Boxes 1, 2, 7   [NYHS]

Provincetown, Massachusetts

Provincetown Museum   [Kinkor]
The Whydah Project

Salt Lake City, Utah

Family History Library
FHL, Reel 395554, "Petition of Eleanor Anderson to the Corporation of Trinity
    House," Trinity House Petitions, vol. 2   [Trinity House Petitions]

Washington, D.C.

National Archives
NA 89, "Letters to the Secretary of the Navy from the African Squadron, 1843–1861,"
    Volumes 82, 105–1150   [LtoSofN]

NEWSPAPERS

Anti-Slavery Reporter, 1845
Bahama Gazette, 1784–1806   [bg]
Barbados Gazette; or, General Intelligencer, 1788–89   [gi]
Barbados Mercury, 1766, 1788   [bm]
Cornwall Chronicle (Montego Bay), 1776–94   [cc]
The Diary and Kingston Daily Advertiser, 1799   [kda]
Essequebo and Demerary Gazette, 1803–07   [dg]
Felix Farley's Bristol Journal, 1749
Georgia Gazette, 1792–96   [Georgia Gazette]
Gore's General Advertiser (Liverpool), 1800   [gga]
Liverpool General Advertiser, 1767–1788   [LGA]
Lloyd's Lists, 1702–4, 1741, 1744, 1747–53, 1755, 1757–58, 1760–77, 1779–1808
    (note that the only location of 1702–4 issues is House of Lords Record Office and
    that number after "LL" for these years refers to issue number)   [LL or LList]
Manchester Mercury, 1754–55
Read's Weekly Journal, 1734
Royal Gazette (Kingston), 1780–84, 1792–1800   [kg]
Royal Gazette and Bahama Advertiser, 1804–07   [rg]
Salem Gazette, 1785   [Salem Gazette]
Semanario de Agricultura, Industria y Commercio, 1802–07   [sem]
South Carolina Gazette, 1772
St. George's Chronicle, and New Grenada Gazette, 1792   [stg]
Universal Spectator, 1731
Williamson's Daily Advertiser (Liverpool), 1781–87   [w]

PUBLISHED SOURCES

Adams, John, *Sketches Taken During Ten Voyages to Africa, Between the Years 1786 and
    1800...* (London, 1822)   [Adams]

African Institution, *Fifth Report of the Directors of the African Institution* (London, 1811).

African Institution, *Sixth Report of the Directors of the African Institution* (London, 1812).

African Institution, *Seventh Report of the Directors of the African Institution* (London, 1813).

African Institution, *Eighth Report of the Directors of the African Institution* (London, 1814).

African Institution, *Ninth Report of the Directors of the African Institution* (London, 1815).

African Institution, *Tenth Report of the Directors of the African Institution* (London, 1816).

African Institution, *Eleventh Report of the Directors of the African Institution* (London, 1817).

African Institution, *Twelfth Report of the Directors of the African Institution* (London, 1818).

African Institution, *Thirteenth Report of the Directors of the African Institution* (London, 1820).

African Institution, *Fourteenth Report of the Directors of the African Institution* (London, 1821).

African Institution, *Fifteenth Report of the Directors of the African Institution* (London, 1822).

African Institution, *Eighteenth Report of the Directors of the African Institution* (London, 1825).

African Institution, *Nineteenth Report of the Directors of the African Institution* (London, 1826).

Akinjogbin, I.A., "Archibald Dalzel: Slave Trader and Historian of Dahomey," *Journal of African History*, 7 (1966): 67–78.

Annual Register, 1762, 1792.   [AR]

Anon, *Gentleman's Magazine*, October, 1773 [GentMag.Oct1773,523]

Anon, *Pertinent en Waarachtig Verhaal van alle de Handelingen en Directie van Pedro van Belle ontrent Den Slavenhandel...* (Rotterdam, 1689)   [Pertinent en Waarachtig Verhaal]

Anon, "The Adventure of the 'Mongovo George'," *Gentleman's Magazine,* 300 (1906):18–26   [GM,1906]

Anon, *Report of the Lords Committee of Council appointed for the Consideration of all Matters Relating to Trade and Foreign Plantations* (London, 1789).   [RL]

Appleby, John C., "A Guinea Venture c. 1657: A Note on the Early English Slave Trade," *Mariner's Mirror*, 79 (1993): 84–7.

Appleby, John C., "'A Business of Much Difficulty': A London Slaving Venture, 1651–54," *Mariner's Mirror*, 83 (1995): 3–14.

Armstrong, James C., "Madagascar and the Slave Trade in the Seventeenth Century," *Omaly Sy Anio*, 17–20 (1983–84): 211–32.

Astley, T. (ed.), *A New General Collection of Voyages and Travels: Consisting of the Most Esteemed Relations Which Have Been Hitherto Published in Any Language*, 4 vols. (London, 1745–47).

Behrendt, Stephen D., "The Journal of an African Slaver, 1789–1792, and the Gold Coast Slave Trade of William Collow," *History in Africa*, 22 (1995): 61–71.

Benezet, Anthony, *Some Historical Account of Guinea* (London, 1788).

Bethell, Leslie, *The Abolition of the Brazilian Slave Trade* (Cambridge, 1970).

Biblioteca Nacional do Rio de Janeiro, *Documentos Históricos da Biblioteca Nacional do Rio de Janeiro*, 110 vols. (Rio de Janeiro, 1929–55), vols. 61, 62. [Documentos]

Boeseken, A.J., *Slaves and Free Blacks at the Cape, 1658–1700* (Capetown, 1977).

Boudriot, Jean, *Traite et Navire Négrier: L'Aurore* (Paris, 1984)

British and Foreign Anti-Slavery Society, *Slave Traders in Liverpool* (London, 1862). [Brit&FgnAnti]

Brodhead, John Romeyn, *Documents Relative to the Colonial History of New York*, 10 vols. (New York, 1853–60), vols. 2, 5. [DCHSNY]

Buffet, Henri-François, *Vie et Société au Port-Louis des Origines à Napoleon III* (Rennes, 1972).

Butterworth, William, pseud for Henry Schroeder, *Three Years Adventures of a Minor* (Leeds, 1822).

Carreira, António, *As Companhias Pombalinas: de Grão-Pará e Maranhão e Pernambuco e Paraíba*, 2nd edition (Lisbon, 1983)

Catterall, Helen Tunnicliff (ed.), *Judicial Cases Concerning American Slavery and the Negro,* 5 vols. (Washington, 1926–37), vols. 1 and 2.

Clarkson, Thomas, *History of the Rise, Progress, and Accomplishment of the Abolition of the African Slave Trade by the British Parliament*, 3 vols. (London, 1808)

Corry, Joseph, *Observations upon the Windward Coast of Africa* (London, 1807)

Coughtry, Jay, *The Notorious Triangle: Rhode Island and the African Slave Trade, 1700–1807* (Philadelphia, 1981)

Craig, Robert and Rupert Jarvis, (eds.) *Liverpool Registry of Merchant Ships* (Manchester, 1967) [Craig]

Crooks, J.J. (ed.), *Records Relating to the Gold Coast Settlements from 1750 to 1874* (London, 1923)

Memoirs of the Late Captain Hugh Crow of Liverpool (London, 1830) [crow]

Cultru, P. (ed.), *Premier Voyage du Sieur de la Courbe fait à la Coste d'Afrique en 1689* (Paris, 1913)

Daget, Serge, *Répertoire des Expéditions Négrières Françaises à la Traite Illégale (1814–1850)* (Nantes, 1988).

Dalleo, Peter D., "Africans in the Caribbean: A Preliminary Reassessment of Recaptives in the Bahamas, 1811–1860," *Journal of the Bahamas Historical Society*, 6 (1984): 15–24.

D'Auvergne, Edmund B., *Human Livestock*, (London, nd).

Davenant, Charles, *The Political and Commercial Works of that Celebrated Writer Charles D'avenant . . .*, 5 vols. (London, 1771), vol. 5

Davis, Ralph, *The Rise of the English Shipping Industry in Seventeenth and Eighteenth Centuries* (London, 1962).

Defoe, Daniel, *History of the Pirates* (London, 1814). Reprint of 1724 edition.

De Studer, Elena F. S., *Trata de Negros en el Rio de la Plata Durante el Siglo XVII* (Montevideo, 1984)

Dodson, John, *A Report of the Case of the Louis* (London, 1817)

Donnan, Elizabeth, (ed.) *Documents Illustrative of the History Slave Trade to America*, 4 vols. (Washington, D.C. 1930–33) [Donnan]

Donnan, Elizabeth, "The Early Days of the South Sea Company, 1711–1718," *Journal of Economic and Business History*, 2 (1929): 419–50. [Donnan,"SouthSeaCo"]

Dow, George Francis, *Slave Ships and Slaving* (Salem, Massachusetts, 1927)

Durnford, Charles, and Edward Hyde East, *Term Reports in the Court of King's Bench*, 5 vols. (London, 1817), vol. 5.

Edwards, Bryan, *A Speech Delivered at a Free Conference Between the Honourable Council and Assembly of Jamaica* (Kingston, 1789)

Edgar, Walter (ed.), *The Letterbook of Robert Pringle 1737–45*, 2 vols, (Columbia, South Carolina, 1972) [PringleLB]

Elder, Melinda, *The Slave Trade and the Economic Development of Eighteenth Century Lancaster* (Halifax, 1992)

Eltis, David, "The British Trans-Atlantic Slave Trade after 1807," *Journal of Maritime History*, 4 (1974): 1–11

Emmer, Pieter C., "De Laatste Slavenreis van de Middelburgsche Commercie Compagnie," *Economisch en Sociaal-Historisch Jaarboek*, 34 (1971): 72–123

English Reports, 169 (1845) [English Reports]

The Federal Cases, 30 vols. (St. Paul, Minnesota, 1894–7) [Federal cases]

Ford, Amelia C (ed.), "An Eighteenth Century Letter from a Sea Captain to his Owner," *New England Quarterly*, 3 (1930): 136–45 [NewEnglandQuart]

Forde, Daryll, (ed.) *Efik Traders of Old Calabar: Containing the Diary of Antera Duke* (London, 1956)

Ford, W.C. (ed.), *The Commerce of Rhode Island, 1726–1800*, 2 vols. (Massachusetts Historical Society, 1914–15) ["Commerce of Rhode Island"]

Froger, François, *A Relation of a Voyage made in the year 1695, 1696, 1697* (London, 1698)

Galenson, David, *Traders, Planters and Slaves: Market Behaviour in Early English America* (Cambridge, 1986).

Gaspar, David Barry, *Bondmen and Rebels: A Study of Master–Slave Relations in Antigua* (Baltimore, 1985).

Gehring, Charles T. and Schiltkamp, J.A. (eds.), *Curacao Papers, 1640–1665: New Netherlands Documents, XIV* (Interlaken, 1987). O'Callaghan, E.B., *Voyages of the Slavers St. John and Arms of Amsterdam, 1659, 1663; together with Additional Papers Illustrative of the Slave trade Under the Dutch* (Albany, 1867).

Gill, Conrad, *Merchants and Mariners of the Eighteenth Century* (London, 1961).

Liverpool Directory (Liverpool, 1807).

Great Britain, *Acts of the Privy Council*, vols. III, VI

Great Britain, *Calendar of State Papers: Colonial Series* (London, 1878–1905) vols. 1, 5, 7–21, 42 [CSPCS]

Great Britain, *Commons' Journal*, 1738–39 [CJ,1738–39]

Great Britain, *Irish University Press Series of British Parliamentary Papers: Slave Trade*, vols. 1–90 (Shannon, 1969–72) [IUP,ST]

Great Britain, *Journal of the Commissioners of Trade and Plantations preserved in the Public Record Office 1704–1782*, 14 vols. (London, 1920–37). [JBT]

Great Britain, *Journal of the House of Lords*, XVIII

Great Britain, *Manuscripts of the House of Lords: New Series*, 11 vols. (London, 1900) [mssHL]

Great Britain, *Parliamentary Papers* [PP]

1777, IX.
1788, XXII.
1789, XXIV, XXV, XXVI.
1790, XXIX, XXX, XXXI.
1790–91, XXXIV.
1792, XXXV.
1795–96, XLII.
1798–99, XLVIII.
1799 XLVIII.
1801–2, IV.
1803–4, X.
1806, XIII.
1813–14, XII.
1816, VII.
1823, XIX.
1825, XXVII, XXIX.
1826, XXIX.
1826–7, XXVI.
1828, XXVI.
1829, XXVI.
1830, X.
1831, XIX.
1831–32, XLVII.
1842, XLIV.
1845, XLIX.
1847–8, XXII.
1852–3, XXXIX.

Green-Pedersen, Svend E., "The Scope and Structure of the Danish Negro Slave Trade," *Scandinavian Economic History Review*, 19 (1971): 149–97.

Hair, P.E.H., Adam Jones, Robin Law, *Barbot on Guinea: The Writings of Jean Barbot on West Africa, 1678–1712* (London, 1992)   [Barbot]

Hall, Gwendolyn Midlo, *Africans in Colonial Louisiana: The Development of Afro-Creole Culture in the Eighteenth Century* (Baton Rouge, 1992)

Hallett, Robin (ed.), *Records of the African Association, 1788–1831* (London, 1964)

Hawkins, John, *Hawkins' Voyages During the Reigns of Henry VIII, Queen Elizabeth and James I* (London, 1878)

Hernaes, Per O., *Slaves, Danes, and African Coast Society: The Danish Slave Trade from West Africa and Afro-Danish Relations on the Eighteenth Century Gold Coast* (Trondheim, 1995)

Herrera Casasús, Maria Luisa, *Presencia y Esclavitud del Negro en La Huesteca* (México City, 1989)

Historical Manuscripts Commission, *Manuscripts of the Duke of Portland*, 2 vols. (London, 1893)   [HMC]

Holliday, John, *A Short Account of... the Putrid Bilious Fever... which Appeared in the City of Havanna* (Boston, 1796)

Howard, Warren S. *American Slavers and the Federal Law, 1837–1862* (Berkeley, 1963)

Jackson, Roland (ed.), *Journal of a Voyage to Bonny River on the West Coast of Africa* (Letchworth, 1934)

Jeffery, Reginald W. (ed.), *Dyott's Diary, 1781–1845, A Selection from the Journal of William Dyott...*, 2 vols (London, 1907)

Johnson, Vera M., "Sidelights on the Liverpool Slave Trade, 1789–1807," *Mariner's Mirror*, 38 (1952): 276–93

Jones, Adam, *Brandenburg Sources for West African History, 1680–1700* (Stuttgart, 1985).

Justesen, Ole, *Danish Documents Concerning the History of Ghana, 1657–1754* (forthcoming).

Klooster, Wim, *Illicit Riches: The Dutch Trade in the Caribbean, 1648–1795* (Leiden, 1997)

Klooster, Wim, "Slavenvaart op Spaanse Kusten: Der Nederlandse Slavenhandel met Spaans Amerika, 1648–1701," *Tijdschrift voor Zeegeschiedenis*, 16 (1997): 132–5.

Knutsford, Viscountess (ed.), *Life and Letters of Zachary Macaulay* (London, 1900)   [zm]

Kup, Alexander (ed.), *Adam Afzelius. Sierra Leone Journal* (Uppsala, 1967)   [kup]

Lambert, Sheila (ed.), *House of Commons Sessional Papers of the Eighteenth Century*, 145 vols. (Wilmington, Delaware, 1975)

Law Magazine, 25 (1845)

Law, Robin (ed.), *Further Correspondence of the Royal African Company of England Relating to the Slave Coast of Africa, 1681–1699* (Madison, Wisconsin, 1992)

Leibbrandt, H.C.V., *Precis of the Archives of the Cape of Good Hope*, vol. 14, *Journal, 1662–1670* (Cape Town, 1901)

Lewis, Michael, *The Hawkins Dynasty: Three Generations of a Tudor Family* (London, 1969)

Ly, Abdoulaye, *La Compagnie du Sénégal* (Paris, 1958)   [Ly]

Ly, Abdoulaye, *Un Navire de Commerce sur la Côte Sénégambienne en 1685* (Dakar, 1964)   [Ly, "Un Navire de Commerce,"]

Lloyd's Register of Shipping, (London) 1764, 1768, 1776, 1778–84, 1786–1787, 1789–1808.   [LR]

Macau, Jacques, *La Guinée Danoise* (Aix-en-Province, nd, but circa 1967–73)

Manchester, Alan K., *British Preeminence in Brazil: Its Rise and Decline* (Chapel Hill, 1933)

Martin, Bernard, and Martin Spurrell (eds.), *The Journal of a Slave Trader (John Newton), 1750–1754* (London, 1962)

Mason, George C, "The African Slave Trade in Colonial Times," *American Historical Record*, 1 (1872): 311–19, 338–45.   [AmerHistRec]

Mason, William Powell, *A Report of the Case of the Jeune Eugènie* (Boston, 1822)

McLeod, John, *A Voyage to Africa with Some Account of the Manners and Customs of the Dahomian People* (London, 1820)

Mettas, Jean, *Répertoire des Expéditions Négrières Françaises au XVIIIe Siècle;* Tome 1, *Nantes* (Paris, 1978); Tome 2, *Ports Autres que Nantes* (Paris, 1984), eds. Serge and Michèle Daget.

Meyer-Heiselberg, R., *Notes from the Liberated African Department in the Archives at Fourah Bay College, Freetown, Sierra Leone* (Uppsala, 1967)

Minchinton, Walter E., Celia King, and Peter Waite (eds.), *Virginia Slave Trade Statistics, 1698–1775* (Richmond, 1984) [Minch]

Minchinton, Walter E., "The Seaborne Slave Trade of North Carolina," *North Carolina Historical Review*, 71 (1994): 1–61. [Minchinton]

Moore, David D., *Site Report: Historical & Archaeological Investigations of the Shipwreck "Henrietta Marie"* (Key West, Florida, 1997)

Moore, Francis, *Travels to the Inland Parts of Africa* (London, 1737)

Moore, George H., *Notes on the History of Slavery in Massachusetts* (New York, 1968), reprint of 1866 edition [Moore, George]

Morales Carrion, Arturo, *Auge y Decadencia de la Trata Negrera en Puerto Rico (1820–1860)* (San Juan, 1978)

Mouser, Bruce L., "Voyage of the Good Sloop 'Dolphin' to Africa, 1795–1796," *American Neptune*, 38 (1978): 249–61

Moutokias, Zacarias, *Contrabando y Control Colonial en el Siglo XVII Buenos Aires, el Atlantico y el Espacio Peruano* (Buenos Aires, 1988)

Munford, Clarence J., *Black Ordeal of Slavery and Slave Trading in the French West Indies, 1625–1715*, 3 vols. (Lewiston, New York, 1991)

Murray, David, *Odious Commerce: Britain, Spain and the Abolition of the Cuban Slave Trade* (Cambridge, 1980)

Nørregård, Georg, *Danish Settlements in West Africa, 1658–1850* (Boston, 1965)

Palmer, Colin, *Human Cargoes: The British Slave Trade to Spanish America* (Urbana, 1981)

Pinckard, George, *Notes on the West Indies…*, 3 vols.(London, 1806)

Poortvliet, P. F. (ed.), *De Bemanning der Schepen van de Middelburgsche Commercie Compagnie, 1721–1803*, 5 vols. (Zeeland, 1995)

Postma, Johannes Menne, *The Dutch in the Atlantic Slave Trade, 1600–1815* (Cambridge, 1990)

Preciado, Palacio, *La Trata de Negros por Cartagena de Indias, 1650–1750* (Tunja, Colombia, 1972)

Priestley, Margaret, *West African Trade and Coast Society: A Family History* (London, 1969)

Raak, Chris, *Adriaan Jacobze: Slavenhaler in dienst van de Middelburgse Commercie Compagnie, 1750–1770: een biografische benadering van de Nederlandse Slavenhandel* (Amsterdam, 1989)

Richardson, David, *Bristol, Africa and the Eighteenth Century Slave Trade to America*: vol. 1, *The Years of Expansion, 1698–1729* (Bristol, 1986); vol. 2, *The Years of Ascendancy, 1730–1745* (Bristol, 1987); vol. 3, *The Years of Decline, 1746–1769* (Bristol, 1991); vol. 4, *The Final Years, 1770–1807* (Bristol, 1996).

Richardson, David and Maurice M. Schofield, "Whitehaven and the Eighteenth Century British Slave Trade," *Transactions of the Cumberland and Westmorland Antiquarian and Archaeological Society*, 92 (1992): 183–204.

Richardson, David, Kathy Beedham, and M.M. Schofield, *Liverpool Shipping and Trade, 1744–1786* (ESRC Data Archives, University of Essex, 1992) [LST]

Robinson, Walter, *Phyllis Wheatley and her Writings* (New York, 1984).

Roussier, Paul (ed.), *L'Etablissement d'Issiny, 1687–1702: Voyage de DuCasse, Tibierge et Damon à la côte de Guinée* (Paris, 1935)

Liverpool and Slavery: An Historical Account of the Liverpool-African Slave Trade, by a *"Genuine Dicky Sam"* (Liverpool, 1884) [sam]

Sanders, Joanne Mcree, *Barbados Records: Wills and Administrations*, 3 vols. (1979–81)

Schofield, Maurice M., "The Slave Trade from Lancashire and Cheshire Ports Outside Liverpool, circa 1750–circa 1790," in Roger Anstey and P.E.H. Hair (eds.), *Liverpool, the African Slave Trade, and Abolition*, enlarged edition (Liverpool, 1989): 239–81. [Schofield]

Schwarz, Suzanne, *Slave Captain: The Career of James Irvine in the Liverpool Slave Trade* (Wrexham, 1995)

Snelgrave, W., *A New Account of Some Parts of Guinea and the Slave Trade* (London, 1734) [Snelgrave, New Account]

Society of Friends, *Case of the Vigilante, a ship employed in the slave trade* (London, 1823)

Stock, Leo Francis (ed.), *Proceedings and Debates of the British Parliaments Respecting North America*, 5 vols. (Washington, DC., 1924–41).

Svalesen, Lief, *Slaveskipet Fredensborg: og den dansk-norske slavehandel på 1700-tallet* (Oslo, 1996)

Svalesen, Lief, "The Slave Ship 'Fredensborg': History, Shipwreck, and Find," *History in Africa*, 22 (1995): 455–58 [Svalesen, 1995]

Tattersfield, Nigel, *The Forgotten Trade: Comprising the Log of the "Daniel and Henry" of 1700 and Accounts of the Slave Trade from the Minor Ports of England, 1698–1725* (London, 1991)

Taunay, Afonso D'escragnole, "Subsidios para a história do tráfico africano no Brasil Colonial," in Leonardo Dantas Silva (ed.), *Estudos sobre a Escravadão Negra* (Recife, 1988):75–356

Thesée, Françoise, *Les Ibos de l'Amélie: Destinée d'une cargaison de traite clandestin à la Martinique, 1822–28* (Paris, 1986)

Torrington, F. William (ed.), *House of Lords Sessional Papers*, session 1798–99, 3 vols. (Rahway, New Jersey, 1975), Vol. 3

United States, *American State Papers*, Second Series, vol. 5

United States, Congress

Senate Executive Document, Session 26–2, vols. 115, 125; 28–2, 150; 30–1, 28; 30–2, 61; 31–2, 6; 150; 34–1, 99; 35–1, 49; 37–2, 40; 37–2, 53 [SED]

House Executive Document, 27–1, 34; 30–2, 671; 35–2, 104; 36–2, 7 [HED]

House Report, 27–3, 283 [HR]

Uring, N, *The Voyages and Travels of Capt. Nathaniel Uring* (London, 1726)

Van Dantzig, Albert, *The Dutch and the Guinea Coast, 1674–1742: A Collection of Documents from the General State Archive at the Hague* (Accra, 1978) [VanDantzig]

Verger, Pierre, *Trade Relations Between the Bight of Benin and Bahia, 17th to 19th Century*, trans. Evelyn Crawford (Ibadan, 1976)

Villiers, Patrick, *Traite des Noirs et Navires Négriers au XVIIIe Siècle* (Paris, 1987)

Vila Vilar, Enriqueta, *Hispanoamerica y el Comercio de Esclavos* (Seville, 1977).

Wax, Darold, "Negro Imports into Pennsylvania, 1720–1766," *Pennsylvania History*, 32 (1965): 255–87 [Wax, 1965]

Wax, Darold, "A Philadelphia Surgeon on a Slaving Voyage to Africa, 1749–51," *Pennsylvania Magazine of History and Biography*, 92 (1968): 465–93 [Wax, 1968]

Wax, Darold, "Black Immigrants: The Slave Trade in Colonial Maryland," *Maryland Historical Magazine*, 73 (1978): 30–45 [Wax, 1978]

Weeden, William B, "The Early African Slave-Trade in New England," *Proceedings of the American Antiquarian Society*, New Series, 5 (1887): 107–28

Westergaard, Waldemar, *The Danish West Indies Under Company Rule, (1671–1754)* (New York, 1917).

Williams, Gomer, *History of the Liverpool Privateers and Letters of Marque with an Account of the Liverpool Slave Trade* (London, 1897) [gw]

Wood, Peter H., *Black Majority: Negroes in South Carolina from 1670 through the Stono Rebellion* (New York, 1974)

Zook, George Frederick, *The Company of Royal Adventurers Trading to Africa* (Lancaster, Pennsylvania, 1919)

UNPUBLISHED SECONDARY SOURCES

Adderley, Roseanne Marion, "'New Negroes from Africa': Culture and Community Among Liberated Africans in the Bahamas and Trinidad 1810–1900." Unpublished Ph.D. dissertation, University of Pennsylvania, 1996.

Menard, Russell R., "'The Sweet Negotiation of Sugar': Barbados, 1640–1660" (Unpublished paper, 1996).

Priester, L.R., "De Nederlandse houding ten aanzien van de slavenhandel en slavernij, 1596–1863: het gedrag van de slavenhandelaren van de Commercie Compagnie van Middelburg in de 18e eeuw." Unpublished MA thesis, Erasmus University, Rotterdam, 1986.

Stein, Robert Louis, Data set of French slave trading voyages collected by Robert Louis Stein.

APPENDIX B: LIST OF PAPERS DERIVED FROM THE DATA SET

Stephen D. Behrendt, "The Captains in the British Slave Trade from 1785 to 1807," *Transactions of the Historic Society of Lancashire and Cheshire*, 140 (1991): 79–140.

David Eltis and Stanley L. Engerman, "Was the Slave Trade Really Dominated by Men?," *Journal of Interdisciplinary History*, 22 (1992): 237–57.

David Eltis and Stanley L. Engerman, "Fluctuations in Age and Sex Ratios in the Transatlantic Slave Trade, 1663–1864," *Economic History Review*, 2nd series, 46 (1993): 308–23.

David Eltis and Stephen D. Behrendt, "Research Note on the Atlantic Slave Trade Database Project," *Uncommon Sense: Newsletter of the Institute of Early American History and Culture* (Summer 1994).

David Eltis and David Richardson, "Productivity in the Transatlantic Slave Trade," *Explorations in Economic History*, 32 (1995): 465–84.

David Eltis, "The Volume and African Origins of the British Slave Trade before 1714," *Cahiers d'Etudes Africaines*, 138–9 (1995): 617–27.

David Eltis, "The Transatlantic Slave Trade to the British Americas before 1714: Annual Estimates of Volume, Direction and African Origins," in *The Lesser Antilles in the Age of European Expansion*, eds. Robert Paquette and Stanley L. Engerman (Gainesville, Florida, 1996): 182–205.

Stephen D. Behrendt, "The Marketing of African Slaves in the Americas, 1780–1807: Evidence from the British Trade," unpublished paper presented at the Social Science History Association, annual conference (New Orleans, 1996).

Stephen D. Behrendt, "The Transatlantic Slave Trade Database Project, with a Note on African Resistance to the Slave Trade," unpublished paper presented to the W.E.B. Du Bois Institute, Harvard University (April 1997).

David Eltis and David Richardson, "The 'Numbers Game' and Routes to Slavery," in *Slavery and Abolition*, 18, no.1 (April 1997): 1–15, and republished in *Routes to Slavery: Direction, Ethnicity and Mortality in the Transatlantic Slave Trade*, eds. David Eltis and David Richardson (London, 1997).

David Eltis and David Richardson, "West Africa and the Transatlantic Slave Trade: New Evidence of Long-Run Trends," *Slavery and Abolition*, 18, no. 1 (April 1997): 16–35 and republished in *Routes to Slavery*, eds. Eltis and Richardson.

Herbert S. Klein and Stanley L. Engerman, "Long-Term Trends in African Mortality in the Transatlantic Slave Trade," *Slavery and Abolition*, 18, no.1 (April 1997): 36–48, and republished in *Routes to Slavery*, eds., Eltis and Richardson.

Stephen D. Behrendt, "Crew Mortality in the Transatlantic Slave Trade in the Eighteenth Century," *Slavery and Abolition*, 18, no.1 (April 1997): 49–71, and republished in *Routes to Slavery*, eds. Eltis and Richardson.

Philip D. Morgan, "The Cultural Implications of the Atlantic Slave Trade: African Regional Origins, American Destinations and New World Developments," *Slavery and Abolition*, 18, no.1 (April 1997): 122–45, and republished in *Routes to Slavery*, eds. Eltis and Richardson.

Stephen D. Behrendt, "The Annual Volume and Regional Distribution of the British Slave Trade, 1780–1807," *Journal of African History*, 38 (1997): 187–211.

Stephen D. Behrendt and David Eltis, "Competition, Market Power, and the Impact of Abolition on the Transatlantic Slave Trade: Connections between Africa and the Americas," unpublished paper presented at the American Historical Association, annual conference (January 1997).

David Eltis, Stephen D. Behrendt, and David Richardson, "Cooperation and Resistance: African Shaping of the Transatlantic Slave Trade," unpublished paper presented at the Institute of Commonwealth Studies, London (May 1997).

Stephen D. Behrendt, David Eltis, and David Richardson, "The Bights in Comparative Perspective: the Economics of Long-Term Trends in Population Displacement from West and West-Central Africa to the Americas before 1850," unpublished paper presented at the Summer Institute on the African Diaspora from the "Nigerian" Hinterland, York University, Ontario (July 1997).

David Richardson, "Quantifying the Slave Trade: The W.E.B. Du Bois Institute Database," in *Source Material for Studying the Slave Trade and the African Diaspora*, ed. Robin Law, Centre of Commonwealth Studies, University of Stirling, Occasional Papers, no. 5 (1997): 61–8.

David Eltis, David Richardson and Stephen D. Behrendt, "The Structure of the Transatlantic Slave Trade, 1595–1867," in *Transatlantic Passages*, eds. Henry Louis Gates Jr., Carl Pederson, and Maria Diedrich (Oxford University Press, forthcoming).

Stephen D. Behrendt, David Eltis and David Richardson, "Out of Africa: The Origins of Enslaved Africans Entering the Atlantic World, 1660–1809," unpublished paper presented to a conference on "Black Diasporas in the Western Hemisphere," Australian National University, Canberra (April 1998).

Stephen D. Behrendt, David Eltis and David Richardson, "The Volume of the Transatlantic Slave Trade: A Reassessment with Particular Reference to the Portuguese Contribution," unpublished paper presented to the workshop on Brazil and Africa held at Emory University, Atlanta (April 1998).

David Eltis, Paul E. Lovejoy and David Richardson, "Ports of the Slave Trade: An Atlantic-Wide Perspective," unpublished paper presented to the symposium on "Ports of the Slave Trade (Bights of Benin and Biafra)" held at the University of Stirling (June 1998).

Philip D. Morgan and David Eltis (eds.), special issue of the *William and Mary Quarterly* devoted to papers presented at a conference on the new dataset held at Williamsburg, September, 1998. Forthcoming in 2000.

APPENDIX C: CODEBOOK

PORTDEP PORTRET PLACREG PLACCONS DESTIN: ports of departure, etc.

1 Nantes	49 Falmouth
2 Bayonne	50 Bideford
3 Bordeaux	51 Alicante, Spain
4 Brest, France	52 La Coruña
5 Dieppe	53 Cadiz
6 Dunkerque (Dunkirk)	56 Spain, unspecified
7 Gorée, Africa	57 Lisbon
8 Honfleur	58 England, unspecified
10 France (unspecified)	59 Exeter
11 La Rochelle	60 British Americas
12 Le Havre	61 Britain, unspecified
13 Lorient	62 Portsmouth, England
14 Marseille	63 New York
15 Sète, France, see also Cette	64 Boston
16 Morlaix	66 Rhode Island
17 Port-au-Prince	67 Montserrat
18 Rochfort	68 Milford Haven
19 St. Brieuc	70 Whitehaven
20 St. Malo	72 Ile de France
21 Martinique	73 Cape Coast (Africa)
22 Vannes	74 Port-Louis (Mauritius)
24 Dinard	75 Newfoundland
26 Batz (Ile de)	76 Curaçao
28 St. Nazaire	77 Newport, Rhode Island
30 Flessingue (Flesink)	79 St. Christopher
32 Madeira	80 Limerick
33 Saltatudas	82 Stade en Land
34 Lyme	(Groningen/Friedland)
35 Holland unspecified	83 Maryland
36 New England	84 Mindin
37 Amsterdam	87 Carolina
38 Zeeland/Middleburg	88 Virginia
39 Maze (Rotterdam area)	89 Nevis
40 North of Amsterdam	90 Tobago
41 Guernsey	91 Non-British territory
42 Ilfracombe, Devon	92 Leeward Islands
43 Jersey	93 Jamaica
44 Plymouth	94 Antigua
46 Liverpool	95 Dartmouth, Devon
47 Bristol	96 Bermuda
48 London	97 Barbados

98 Africa
101 Cuba, unspecified
104 Havana
105 Santiago de Cuba
106 Trinidad de Cuba
108 Matanzas
109 Canasi
110 Bahia Honda
111 Cabanas
114 Cardenas
116 Guanimar
120 Brazil, unspecified
121 Caracas (Santiago de Leon)
122 Paranaguá
123 Pará
124 Africa from Cape Lopez south
125 Maranhão
126 Catuamo and Maria Farinha
127 Pernambuco
129 Savannah
130 Rio de Janeiro
132 San Domingo
133 Loanda
134 Rotterdam
135 France (Medit coast, unspecified)
140 Macaé
141 Mangaratiba
144 Rio São Jeso
145 St. Catherines
146 Vitória
147 Rio de Janeiro province
152 Santos
153 São Sebastião
156 São Francisco
160 Bahia, unspecified
163 Baltimore, Maryland
165 Charleston, South Carolina
166 Tenerife
167 USA, unspecified
168 New Bedford, USA
169 New Orleans
170 Cayenne
171 St. Martin
172 St. Eustatius
173 St. Thomas

174 Puerto Rico
175 Bristol, Rhode Island
178 Montevideo
179 St. Bartholomew
180 Cape Verde Islands
181 Bissau, Africa
182 Sierra Leone, Africa
183 São Tomé or Princes Island
187 Barcelona
188 Guadaloupe
189 Gibraltar
196 Senegal, Africa
197 Odessa
198 Cork
203 St. Tropez
204 Quimper
205 Paimboeuf
206 Anvers
207 Les Sables
208 Lancaster
209 Cowes
210 Grenada
211 Dominica
212 Demerara
213 Little Compton, Rhode Island
214 Warren, Rhode Island
215 Tiverton, Rhode Island
216 North Kingston, Rhode Island
217 Salem
218 Providence, Rhode Island
219 Newport and Salem
221 Newport and Boston
222 Conway
234 Chester, England
237 Londonderry
242 Greenock
246 Rappahannock, Virginia
248 Poole, Dorset
250 Basse Indres
251 Calais, France
252 Seville
254 Whitby, Yorkshire
255 Yarmouth, Great Yarmouth, Norfolk
256 Hull, Yorkshire

261 North Carolina
262 Hampton, Virginia
270 South Carolina
272 Norfolk County, Virginia
276 Williamsburg, Virginia
279 Philadelphia
281 Massachusetts
282 Massachusetts Bay
284 Newbury (Newburyport), Massachusetts
286 Portsmouth, New Hampshire
292 Patuxent, Maryland
297 New Haven, Connecticut
298 Haddam, Connecticut
307 Kingston, Massachusetts
333 Piel of Foulney
334 Piscataqua
335 Quèbec
336 Glasgow
339 Leith, Scotland
341 Dublin
342 Strangford, Ireland
350 Airth, near Stirling, Scotland
357 Barmouth
362 Connecticut
372 Deptford, London
375 Dungarvan, Ireland
376 Dover, Kent
379 Ringsend, Dublin
383 Folkstone
384 Frodsham, Cheshire
386 Sunbury, Georgia
387 Guildford, Connecticut
388 Gainsborough
396 Ipswich
397 Ireland
398 Point Askaig, Italy
406 Lough Neagh
408 Lindale, Lancashire
409 Rotherhithe, London
411 King's Lynn
412 Amesbury, Massachusetts
413 Arundel, Massachusetts
414 Cohasset, Massachusetts
416 Charlestown, Massachusetts

420 Dighton, Massachusetts
421 Duxbury, Massachusetts
422 Georgetown, Massachusetts
423 Hingham, Massachusetts
430 Marshfield, Massachusetts
434 Scituate, Massachusetts
435 Salisbury, Massachusetts
436 Marblehead, Massachusetts
437 Annapolis, Maryland
443 Pamunkey, Maryland
446 Talbot County, Maryland
449 Biddeford, Maine
450 Berwick, Maine
451 Robbinston, Maine
452 Bath, Maine
453 Rockland, Maine
454 Calais, Maine
455 Freeport, Maine
456 Sheepscutt (river), Maine, formerly Newcastle
457 Camden, Maine
458 Prospect, Maine
459 Richmond, Maine
460 Montrose, Scotland
461 Maryport
464 Bertie County, North Carolina
465 Chowan river, North Carolina
466 Hyde County, North Carolina
469 Roanoke, North Carolina
473 New Jersey
475 New Providence
478 New Shoreham, Sussex
479 Newnham, Gloucester
484 Northam, Devon
486 Norwich
487 Marcus Hook, Pennsylvania
488 Pennsylvania
489 Parkgate near Chester
495 Warren, Rhode Island
497 Ross, Scotland
501 Rye
505 Scarborough
506 Shields
507 Shoreham, Sussex, see also New Shoreham

508 Saltcoats, Scotland
511 St. John, New Brunswick
512 Stockton
514 Stockwith, Nottinghamshire
516 Sunderland
517 Sweden
520 Teignmouth, Devon
521 River Thames
522 Topsham, Devon
527 Elizabeth River, Virginia
533 Northampton County, Virginia
540 Wexford, Ireland
542 Weymouth, Massachusetts
547 Wales, unspecified
549 Non-British location
550 Galway, Ireland
551 Halifax, Nova Scotia
552 Waterford, Ireland
554 Nova Scotia
555 Naples
556 Swansea, Swansey, Massachusetts
557 New London
559 Freetown (North Amer)
560 Mozambique
561 Lima
562 Mauritius
563 Buenos Aires
567 Newcastle (upon Tyne)
568 Sheerness
570 Scotland
571 Chatham
572 Harwich
573 Perth Amboy, New Jersey
575 Virginia, Elizabeth River
576 Tortola
577 Figuera
578 St. Osyth
579 Broadstairs
582 Ramsgate
583 Southampton
584 St. Cruz (St. Croix)
587 Dundee
588 Woodbridge (unknown English port)
589 Birkenhead

592 Portobello
593 Oporto
597 Kingston, Jamaica
598 Delaware
599 Georgia
602 North Shields
603 Isle of Man
605 Colchester, England
607 Montego Bay, Jamaica
609 St. Lucia
612 Denmark unspecified
615 East Indies
616 Bahamas
617 New Brunswick
625 Borrowstounness (Barrow)
628 Calcutta
630 Bridgeport
631 Brixham
632 Cawsand, Devonshire
636 Isle of Wight
638 Portsery (Ireland)
639 Rochester
641 Sidmouth
645 Torbay, Devon
646 Genoa
647 Hamburg, Altona
649 Kinsale (Ireland)
652 Mahone Bay (Canada)
653 Mediterranean
654 Cronstadt
655 Greenwich
656 Wharton
657 Long Island
658 Emden
660 Middleburg, Holland
661 Bergen, Norway
662 Copenhagen
663 Portland, Maine
672 Wiscasset, Maine
673 Wreck
674 Bance (Bance Island), Africa
676 Martha Brae (Jamaica)
677 St. Kitts
679 Padstowe, Cornwall
680 Port Louis, France

681 Kendal
686 Zuider Zee
688 Gothenberg
689 Bilbao
692 St. Augustine
694 Dordrecht
695 Netherlands, unspecified
696 Brookhaven, New York
697 Sag Harbor, New York
698 Milwell, New Jersey
801 British plantations
    (or Plantation)
802 Prize (unknown place)
844 Prize (taken from French—
    unknown place)

845 Prize (taken from Spanish—
    unknown place)
846 Britain unspecified
848 Prize (taken from Dutch—
    unknown place)
902 Portugal
905 Poulton
906 Ravenglass
907 New Hampshire
908 Workington
909 Preston
910 Youghal
911 Chepstow
912 British North American mainland
913 British Caribbean unspecified

PLAC1TRA PLAC2TRA PLAC3TRA EMBPORT EMBPORT2 MAJBUYPT:
place of purchase

2 São Tomé
3 Princes Island
4 Mascarene Islands
5 Casamance
6 Galam
7 Gambia
8 Gorée
9 Portudal
10 Senegambia (no dominant location,
   south to Rio Nunez, exclusive)
11 Albreda
12 Joal, or Saloum River
13 Sénégal
14 Bissau
15 Bananes (Bananas Islands)
16 Bissagos
17 Cacheu
18 Sierra Leone
19 Sherbro
20 Sierra Leone (no dominant location,
   Rio Nunez to Cape Mesurado)
21 Cape Mount
22 Cape Grand Mount
23 Cape Petit Mount
24 Galinhas

25 Loss (Iles de)
26 Scarcies
27 Mano (Manna)
28 Bassa
29 Grand Bassam or Bassam (east of R.
   Assini)
30 Windward Coast (no dominant
   location, Cape Mesurado to Cape
   Palmas)
31 Junk or Little Junk
32 Grand Junk
33 Mesurado, Grand Mesurado
34 Gold Coast (as used by
   French sources—in effect
   Guinea)
35 Petit Mesurado
36 Cess
37 Grand Cess
38 Petit Cess
39 St. Paul
40 Ivory Coast (no dominant location,
   Cape Palmas to Assinie)
41 Sassandra
43 Tabou
44 Drouin

45 Lahou (Cap)
46 Accra
47 Christiansborg
48 Anomabu, Adja, Agga
49 Apam
50 Gold Coast (no dominant location, Assinie to Cape St. Paul)
51 Ardra (Offra)
52 Axim
53 Eva (Gold Coast)
54 Elmina (Amina, Almind)
57 Kormantine
58 Benin
59 Badagry (Apa)
60 Bight of Benin (no dominant location, Cape St. Paul to River Nun)
61 Epe
62 Judah (Gregoy, Ouidah, Whidah, Whydah)
63 Jacquin (Jakin)
64 Keta (Quitta)
65 Porto Novo
66 Lagos, Onim
67 Popo
68 Grand Popo
69 Petit Popo
70 Bight of Biafra (no dominant location, River Nun to Cape Lopez)
71 Gabon
72 Cape Coast
73 Annobon
75 Bonny
76 Calabar
77 Cap Lopez, Pointe Fêtiche
78 Corisco
79 Formosa
80 Congo North (no dominant location, C. Lopez to Congo)
81 Windward + Ivory + Gold + Benin Coasts (If PLAC1TRA = 81 and PLAC2TRA > 0, then trade continued until PLAC2TRA reached)
82 Ivory + Gold Coasts
83 Cabinda

84 Congo (Kicongo, Manikongo)
85 Loango
86 Malembo (Melimba)
87 Mayoumba (Mayomba)
88 Ambriz
89 Benguela
90 Angola (no single place, could be south and north of Congo pre-1800)
91 Luanda
92 Ibo
93 Kilwa
94 Kerimba
95 Madagascar
96 Mozambique
97 Mombasa or Zanzibar
100 Cape Coast Castle
101 Cape Coast Castle and Windward
102 New Calabar
103 Alampo (Alampi) (East of Accra)
105 Cape Verde Islands
107 Quaqua (Bight of Biafra)
108 Wiamba (Winnebah)
109 Andony (east of Bonny)
113 Apollonia
206 Bance Island
207 Rio Bramiah
208 Ben's Island
209 Rio Bolola
210 Dixcove
213 Rio Pongo
216 Rio Nunez
221 Little Bassa
222 Grand Bassa
223 Sestos (New, Young, Little)
224 Trade Town
226 Sestos (Grand and Rock)
227 Rio Sinou (Liberian coast)
238 Rio Volta
239 Bights, unspecified
249 Rio Nun
250 Cape of Good Hope
254 Cameroons, unspecified
255 Cameroons River
256 Bimbia
259 R. Brass / Brass River

269 Kilongo
274 Nova Redonda
275 Salinas
276 Cape St. Martha
278 Quicombo
279 Coanza R.
281 Lourenço Marques
282 Inhambane
283 Quilimane
285 St. Catherines
286 Sofala, Sofola
287 Pomba, Monfia
288 Anghoza River and island
289 South-east Africa
   unspecified
290 Zanzibar
291 Côte de Malaguette
294 Cap des Palmes
295 Sugary
298 Touau-Toro (unknown)
299 Iles Plantain
303 Costa da Mina
305 James Fort
307 Tantumquerry
309 Windward Coast (Rio Nunez to
   Rio Assini inclusive)
310 Danish Gold Coast
314 Delagoa (Sierra Leone)
317 Madeira
320 Settra Krou
322 Alecuba (Angola)
324 Bessore
325 Barabalemo (near Bonny)
326 Batoa (Windward Coast)
327 Cape Baxos
332 Cacandia (between Nunez and
   Pongas)

333 Casnasonis (unknown)
334 Causacoo (near Gaboon river)
335 Foche (near Calabar?)
336 Fockey (near New Calabar)
337 Garroway Roads
340 Grenada Point, Angola
341 Iron Point, Angola
342 Lamo River (Bight of Benin)
344 Legas, Legis, Legos (Bight of Benin)
346 Ningo (Gold Coast)
347 Cape Mole (Angola?)
349 Cape Padroon (Congo River)
350 Lagoo, Lagoe (Gold Coast)
351 Liverpool River, Angola
353 Metrueba
354 Sekondi, Succondee
355 Siraboom (probably Windward
   Coast)
356 Rio Nazareth
357 Bundy (Bight of Biafra)
360 Cape Logas
361 Senegambia or Sierra Leone
370 Forke
371 Bunby
377 Ambona, Annabona (near Congo)
378 Bilbay, probably Bight of Biafra
379 Bomara (Congo)
382 Timbeys (Gabon)
383 Dembia or Demby River
384 River Kissey (north of Sierra Leone)
389 Tenerife
392 River del Rey
396 Liverpool River, near Nazareth
397 Ile de France
398 Amokou
399 Aghway
400 Penido (unknown)

SLA1PORT ARRPORT ADPSALE1 ADPSALE2 MAJSELPT: place of disembarkation, etc.

2 Mauritius
3 Africa (non-British)
4 Essequibo
5 Berbice
6 Guiana
7 Curaçao
8 Spanish American Mainland
9 St. Eustatius

10 Cape of Good Hope
11 Cayenne
12 Oyapock (Guyane)
13 Bermuda
14 British North American mainland, unspecified
15 Marie-Galante
16 Guadeloupe
19 Pointe-à-Pitre
20 Maryland
21 Martinique
22 Fort-Royale
23 St. Pierre (Fort)
26 St. Domingue
28 Arcahaye
29 Cap (Le) (Cap Français)
30 Cayes (Les) (Caye-St.-Louis, St. Louis)
31 Cul-de-Sac
32 Fort Dauphin
33 Jacmel
34 Jérémie
35 Léogane
36 Petit-Goâve
37 Port-au-Prince
38 Port-de-Paix
39 St. Marc
40 Kingston, Jamaica
41 Montego Bay, Jamaica
42 Port Maria, Jamaica
43 Antonia, Jamaica
45 Port Royal, Jamaica
46 Savanna la Mar (Jamaica)
48 Trinidad
49 Tortola
50 King's Harbour
51 Antigua
52 Barbados
54 Grenada
55 Jamaica
56 Montserrat
57 St. Lucia
58 Tobago
59 Nevis
60 British Caribbean, unspecified
61 French Caribbean, unspecified
63 New York
64 Boston
68 Caribbean, unspecified
69 Spanish Americas
71 Bourbon (including St. Denis)
72 Ile de France
73 St. Croix (Santa Cruz)
74 New Providence
75 Bahamas
76 Demerara
78 Dominica
80 St. Vincent
82 Biloxi, Mississippi
83 Florida
84 Louisiana
85 Norfolk
86 New Orleans
87 Savannah
88 Virginia
89 South Carolina
90 St. Kitts
91 Buenos Ayres, La Plata
92 Cartagena (Columbia)
93 Puerto Rico
94 Portobello (Panama)
95 Paramaribo
96 Surinam
97 Vera Cruz
101 Cuba, unspecified
102 Cuba, south coast
103 Cuba, west coast
104 Havana
105 Santiago de Cuba
106 Trinidad de Cuba
107 Isla de Pinos
108 Matanzas
109 Canasi
110 Bahia Honda
111 Cabanas
112 Mariel
113 Vanes
114 Cardenas
115 Puerto Padre-Puerto Principe
116 Guanimar

117 Sagua
118 Magari, Manzanillo
119 Varana Nueva, San Juan de los Remedios
120 Brazil, unspecified
121 Nuevitas, Cuba
122 Paranaguá
123 Pará
124 Province of Alagoas
125 Maranhão
126 Catuamo and Maria Farinha
127 Pernambuco
128 Ilha Itamarica
129 Porto dos Gallinoa (unknown, probably near Pernambuco)
130 Rio de Janeiro
131 Baia Botafogo
132 Baia Sepetiba
133 Cabo Frio
134 Campos
135 Copacabana
136 Ilha dos Palmas
137 Ilha Grande
138 Ilha Marambaia
139 Ilha Paqueta
140 Macaé
141 Mangaratiba
142 Marica
143 Parati
144 Rio São Jeso
146 Vitório
147 Rio de Janeiro province
148 Taipu
149 Ponte Negra
150 Cabo de Buzios
151 Cananeia
152 Santos
153 São Sebastião
154 Ubatuba
155 Ilha Lobes
158 Rio Grande do Sul Province
159 Rio de Janeiro, São Paulo, Santa Catharina, unspecified
160 Bahia, unspecified
161 Rio Real

162 Pôrto Seguro
163 Maceió
171 Nassau
173 St. Thomas
177 Colonia de Sacramento (north of Montevideo)
178 Montevideo
179 British colony in the Americas other than Bahamas (post-1833)
180 Hispaniola
188 Dutch Americas, unspecified
189 Danish Americas, unspecified
190 Unknown, probably Cuba
191 Unknown, probably Brazil
193 Dois Rios (Rio de Janeiro province)
198 Georgia
199 St. Augustine
200 Charleston
201 St. Maarten
202 Black River, Jamaica
203 Annotta Bay, Jamaica
205 St. Ann's Bay, Jamaica
206 Falmouth, Jamaica
207 Lucea, Jamaica
213 Philadelphia
222 Margarita (Venezuela)
223 Santo Domingo
224 Rio de la Hacha (Venezuela)
240 St. Barthélemy
241 Monte Christi (St. Domingue)
243 Honduras
246 Rappahannock, Virginia
247 South Potomac, Virginia
248 Upper James, Virginia
249 York River, Virginia
250 Vatt (Unknown)
252 West Indies
253 North Carolina
257 Providence, Rhode Island
260 Barbados or Jamaica
262 Hampton, Virginia
264 Antigua or Dominica
266 Dominica or Jamaica
268 Jamaica or St. Kitts

270 Kingston, Savannah, Maryland
275 Martha Brae, Jamaica
276 Spanishtown, Jamaica
277 Orinoko
278 Rhode Island
281 Lower James, Virginia
282 Potomac, Virginia
300 French Africa (Sénégal or Gorée)
302 Beaufort, South Carolina
304 British Leewards
305 Piscataquay
307 Bristol, England
308 Carolina, unspecified
311 Caracas
312 Cumingsberg, Demerara
313 Kingston, Demerara
314 Stabroek, Demerara
315 Morant Bay, Jamaica
316 La Guiara (Venezuela)
319 Môle St. Nicolas, St. Domingue
320 Spanish West Indies
321 Lisbon
322 Cadiz
323 France

331 Leeward Islands
332 St. Pierre, Martinique
337 United States, unspecified
338 Edentown, North Carolina
339 Roanoke
400 Delaware River, New Jersey
401 Eastern New Jersey
402 Mississippi
403 Pensacola
404 Mosquito Shore
440 New Spain
441 Newport, Rhode Island
442 Anguilla
461 Santa Cruz (North Cuba)
471 Sierra Leone
472 Cape Coast Castle
473 St. Helena
474 St. Paul de Loanda
475 Fernando Po
476 Liberia
477 Americas
479 Campeche (Yucatan)
480 Chesapeake
482 Venezuela

FATE: fate of vessel

01 Completed voyage as intended
02 Shipwrecked or destroyed, before slaves embarked
03 Shipwrecked or destroyed, after embarkation of slaves or during slaving
04 Shipwrecked or destroyed, after disembarkation
05 Shipwrecked or destroyed, unspecified
06 Captured by pirates or privateers—before slaves embarked
07 Captured by pirates or privateers—after embarkation of slaves
08 Captured by pirates or privateers—after disembarkation
09 Captured by pirates or privateers—unspecified
10 Captured by British—before slaves embarked
11 Captured by British—after embarkation of slaves
12 Captured by British—after disembarkation of slaves
13 Captured by British—unspecified
14 Captured by Spanish—before slaves embarked
15 Captured by Spanish—after embarkation of slaves
16 Captured by Spanish—after disembarkation of slaves
17 Captured by Spanish—unspecified

18 Captured by Dutch—before slaves embarked
19 Captured by Dutch—after embarkation of slaves
20 Captured by Dutch—after disembarkation of slaves
21 Captured by Dutch—unspecified
22 Captured by Portuguese—before slaves embarked
23 Captured by Portuguese—after embarkation of slaves
24 Captured by Portuguese—after disembarkation of slaves
25 Captured by Portuguese—unspecified
26 Captured, unspecified
27 Condemned—before slaves embarked
28 Condemned—after embarkation of slaves
29 Condemned—Americas after disembarkation of slaves
30 Condemned—unspecified
39 Destroyed—unspecified
40 Sold
41 Left coast with trading cargo intact
42 Taken by Africans
43 Captured by Compagnie du Sénégal
44 Abandoned and/or sold off Africa
45 Captured, unspecified, before slaves embarked
46 Captured, unspecified, after embarkation of slaves
47 Captured, unspecified, after slaves disembarked
48 Captured by pirates—slaves sold in Americas from another ship
49 Sold slaves in Americas—subsequent fate unknown
50 Captured by the French—before slaves embarked
51 Captured by the French—after embarkation of slaves
52 Captured by the French—after slaves disembarked
53 Captured by the French—unspecified
54 Condemned in the Americas by British after slaves disembarked
55 Pressed into government service
56 Captured by slaves: ship did not reach the Americas
57 Captured by crew: fate unknown
58 Condemned in the Americas by British before slaves disembarked
59 Bought at least one slave in Africa—subsequent fate unknown
66 Destroyed, lost or sold as result of slave rebellion
67 Taken, retaken and salvaged before reaching African trade site
68 Sold in the Americas after disembarking slaves
69 Cut off by Africans from shore, ship did not reach the Americas
70 Sold in the Americas—not known whether ship brought slaves
71 Captured before disembarking slaves; vessel recaptured or released subsequently
72 Driven off the African coast with slaves on board
73 Captured by slaves, unknown outcome
74 Captured by crew, did not land slaves in the Americas
75 Lost before Americas: slaves reached port in other ships

 76 Some slaves removed by pirates/privateers
 77 Arrived in Africa, subsequent fate unknown
 78 Captured and recaptured after disembarking slaves
 79 Crew mutiny, slaves landed in the Americas
 80 Cut off by Africans from shore, recaptured and landed slaves in Americas
 81 Captured by slaves, recaptured and landed slaves in the Americas
 82 Captured by slaves, recaptured and landed slaves in the Americas, then lost
 91 Condemned in Africa with slaves, slaves transhipped/sold
 92 Returned direct to Africa after bringing slaves to the Americas
 93 Returned to Europe or Americas without obtaining slaves
 94 Laid up (disarmed) or broken up in Africa
 95 Laid up (disarmed) or broken up in the Americas
 97 Abandoned or condemned for unseaworthiness in the Americas
102 Vice-Admiralty Court, St. Helena, condemned
103 Vice-Admiralty Court, St. Helena, restored
104 Vice-Admiralty Court, British Guiana, condemned
105 Vice-Admiralty Court, British Guiana, restored
106 Vice-Admiralty Court, Cape of Good Hope, condemned
107 Vice-Admiralty Court, Cape of Good Hope, restored
108 Vice-Admiralty Court, Jamaica, condemned
109 Vice-Admiralty Court, Jamaica, restored
110 Vice-Admiralty Court, Sierra Leone, condemned
111 Vice-Admiralty Court, Sierra Leone, restored
112 Vice-Admiralty Court, Barbados, condemned
113 Vice-Admiralty Court, Barbados, restored
114 Vice-Admiralty Court, Mauritius, condemned
115 Vice-Admiralty Court, Mauritius, restored
118 High Court of Admiralty, condemned
119 High Court of Admiralty, restored
120 Court of Mixed Commission, Sierra Leone, condemned
121 Court of Mixed Commission, Sierra Leone, restored
122 Court of Mixed Commission, Havana, condemned
123 Court of Mixed Commission, Havana, restored
124 Court of Mixed Commission, Rio de Janeiro, condemned
125 Court of Mixed Commission, Rio de Janeiro, restored
126 Court of Mixed Commission, Luanda, condemned
127 Court of Mixed Commission, Luanda, restored
128 Court of Mixed Commission, Cape of Good Hope, condemned
129 Court of Mixed Commission, Cape of Good Hope, restored
130 Lagos, Vice-Admiralty Court, condemned
132 Vice-Admiralty Court, Antigua, condemned
134 Vice-Admiralty Court, Tortola, condemned
135 Vice-Admiralty Court, Tortola, restored
138 Vice-Admiralty Court, unspecified, condemned

139 Vice-Admiralty Court, unspecified, restored
141 Given up to the United States government
142 Arrested by Brazil or given up to the Brazilian government
144 Vice-Admiralty Court, Dominica, condemned
148 Vice-Admiralty Court, Bahamas, condemned
149 Vice-Admiralty Court, Bahamas, restored
153 Captured and released without court proceedings
154 Driven or run on shore in the Americas: no court proceedings
155 Given up to the Mexican Government, Vera Cruz
156 Taken to Genoa and given to Sardinian authorities
157 Abandoned in Europe after completing voyage
160 Captured by United States before slaves embarked
161 Captured by United States with slaves
162 Captured by United States after slaves disembarked
163 Captured by United States, slave presence unspecified
164 French proceedings initiated in Africa, acquittal
165 French proceedings initiated in Africa, condemned
166 French proceedings initiated in Africa, unknown outcome
170 French proceedings, initiated in unknown location, acquittal
171 French proceedings, initiated in unknown location, condemned
172 French proceedings, initiated in unknown location, unknown outcome
173 French proceedings initiated in Guadeloupe, acquittal
174 French proceedings initiated in Guadeloupe, condemned
175 French proceedings initiated in Guadeloupe, unknown outcome
176 French proceedings initiated in Martinique, acquittal
177 French proceedings initiated in Martinique, condemned
178 French proceedings initiated in Martinique, unknown outcome
179 French proceedings initiated in Cayenne, acquittal
180 French proceedings initiated in Cayenne, condemned
181 French proceedings initiated in Cayenne, unknown outcome
182 French proceedings initiated in France, acquittal
183 French proceedings initiated in France, condemned
184 French proceedings initiated in France, unknown outcome
185 Detained and condemned in the United States after slaves disembarked

NPAFTTRA: ports of call after leaving trade site

01 Corisco and Princes Island
02 São Tomé
03 Princes Island
04 Bourbon
05 Casamance
10 Cape of Good Hope
11 Annobon
15 Fernando Po and Cameroons

20 Ascension/Assomption
30 Princes Island and Cape Lopez
40 Princes Island and São Tomé
50 São Tomé and Annobon
53 Cape Verde Island
60 Judah, Epee, Princes Island, and Annobon
70 Ile Ste Catherine (Portuguese)
72 Ile de France
80 São Tomé and Cape Lopez
81 Princes Island and Annobon
90 Judah and Princes Island
93 Cape Coast Castle
94 St. Helena
95 Cape Lopez
97 Epee and Princes Island
98 Fernando Po and Princes Island

DATEPL: definition of date of departure

1 Invoice date at port of departure
2 Date of sailing from port of departure—London or Gravesend in British case
3 Departure from Downs (British)
4 Cleared from Custom House
10 Date bond given
12 Date of hiring (Morice papers)
13 Date of purchase of protection against impressment
14 Date Pass issued (Mediterranean Pass in British case)
15 Date of vessel registration
16 Date of sailing orders
17 Date of last crew entry (muster rolls, Seamen's Sixpence records)

RIG: rig of vessel

1 brig
2 schooner (escuna)
3 corvetta
4 ship
5 schooner-brig
6 smack
7 patacho
8 brigantine
9 barque
10 polacca schooner
11 pailebot
12 pilot boat
13 sumaca
14 yacht

15 felucca
16 galliot
17 cutter
18 pinnace
19 launch
20 barqua
21 navio mercante
22 charrua de guerra
23 chalupa
24 pollaca
25 galera
26 vessel
27 sloop
28 steamer
29 whaler
30 fregat
31 barque (Dutch)
32 fluit
33 brik
34 hoeker
35 snauw
36 yaght
37 pinas
38 galjoot
39 hekboot
40 bergantim
41 penque
42 não
43 corsário
44 charrua
45 fregata
46 charruainha
47 balandra
48 paquête
49 hyate (iate)
50 berlin
51 galeta
52 lugger
53 ketch
54 "billd" (Liverpool data) bilander
55 boat (Liverpool data)
56 shallop (Liverpool data)
57 pink
58 hay
59 dogger

60 buque (Portuguese)

TONTYPE: definition of ton used in tonnage

1 Portuguese
2 Brazilian
3 Spanish
4 French
5 United States of America
6 Uruguayan
7 Dutch
8 Hanse Towns (19th Century), Brandenburg
9 Argentinian
10 Swedish
12 Danish
13 English (1786–1835)
14 English (*Statutes at Large,* 5 and 6 Will. IV c. 56, section 6)
15 English (17 and 18 Vic. c. 104, section 22)
16 Chilean
17 England (8 and 9 Vic. c. 89, section 19)
18 Sardinian
19 Norwegian
20 Mexican
21 English (Royal African Company measurement)
22 English (official, pre-1786)

INSURREC: conflict between Africans and Europeans

1 Insurrection on board
2 European vessel cut off from the African coast
3 European vessel's boats cut off from the African coast
4 Source uses term "cut-off" without clear indication of "1" or "2"

NATIONAL NATINIMP: country where vessel registered

1 Portuguese
2 Brazilian
3 Spanish
4 French
5 United States of America
6 Uruguayan
7 Dutch
8 Hanse Towns (19th Century), Brandenburg
9 Argentinian
10 Swedish
11 Russian
12 Danish

13 English
18 Sardinian
19 Norwegian
20 Mexican

DEPTREG RETRNREG CONSTREG REGISREG REGDIS1
REGDIS2 REGDIS3 REGARRP MAJSELRG
MJSELIMP: groupings of ports

1 France
2 Britain
3 Netherlands
4 Spain
5 Portugal
6 Denmark
7 Rhode Island
8 Non RI New England
9 Maryland
10 Virginia
11 Carolinas
12 Georgia
13 Mississippi Delta
14 New York
15 Pennsylvania, Delaware, New Jersey
16 Guadeloupe
17 Canada
18 Dutch Caribbean
19 Off-shore Atlantic: Cape Verde Islands, Azores, Canary Islands
20 Spanish Americas
21 Martinique
22 Guianas
23 Rio de la Plata
24 Virgin Islands
25 St. Domingue
26 North-east Brazil
27 Pernambuco
29 Bahamas
30 South-east Brazil
31 San Domingo
32 Puerto Rico
33 USA (unspecified)
35 Florida
48 Trinidad
51 Antigua
52 Barbados

54 Grenada
55 Jamaica
56 Montserrat
57 St. Lucia
58 Tobago
59 Nevis
60 Bahia
61 Senegambia
62 Sierra Leone
63 Gold Coast
64 Windward Coast
65 Angola
66 South-east Africa (and Cape of Good Hope)
67 Indian Ocean islands
78 Dominica
80 St. Vincent
90 St. Kitts
98 Cuba
99 Not specified

YEAR5: five-year grouping in which voyage occurred

Years 1526–30 = 1 through to Years 1866–70 = 69

YEAR25: quarter-century during which voyage occurred

Years 1526–50 = 1 through Years 1851–75 = 14

REGEM1 REGEM2 REGEM3 EMBREG EMBREG2 MAJBUYRG
MAJBYIMP: regions of embarkation

1 Senegambia
2 Sierra Leone
3 Gold Coast
4 Bight of Benin
5 Bight of Biafra
6 West-central Africa
7 Windward Coast
8 South-east Africa
9 Unknown

FATE2: regrouping of outcome of voyage from
standpoint of slaves

1 Slaves disembarked Americas
2 No slaves embarked
3 Slaves disembarked in Africa/Europe
4 Slaves perished with ship
5 Slaves embarked, transhipped or no further record

6 No information on slaves

FATE3: regrouping of outcome of voyage from standpoint of captor

1 Natural hazard
2 pirate/privateer action
3 British captor
4 Spanish captor
5 Dutch captor
6 Portuguese captor
7 Fleming captor
8 French captor
9 United States captor
10 African captor
11 Crew action
12 Brazil captor
13 Captor unspecified
14 Voyage completed as intended
15 Unknown

FATE4: outcome of voyage from standpoint of owner

1 Delivered slaves for original owners
2 Original goal thwarted (natural hazard)
3 Original goal thwarted (human agency)
4 Unknown outcome

REGDIS11: grouping of first regions of disembarkation (for those voyages with two or more places of disembarkation)

2 Caribbean west of Hispaniola and mainland North America
3 Caribbean east of, and including, Hispaniola

REGDIS21: groupings of second region of disembarkation (for those voyages with two or more places of disembarkation)

1 North America north of Maryland
2 North Americas south of Maryland, St. Domingue, Cuba, Jamaica
3 Maryland, Florida, Eastern Caribbean

DEPTREG1 MJSELRG1: regions of departure or disembarkation of slaves broadly defined

1 Europe
2 United States
3 Caribbean
4 Other Americas
5 Brazil
6 Africa

VARIABLES

(Format key: "F" = numeric; "A" = alphabetic; "6" = six columns wide; "6.4" = six columns wide with four decimal places)

DATA VARIABLES

VOYAGEID Unique identity number
Format: F6

SHIPNAME Shipname
Format: A40

CAPTAINA First captain of ship
Format: A40

CAPTAINB Second captain of ship
Format: A40

CAPTAINC Third captain of ship
Format: A40

PORTDEP Port of departure
Format: F3

DATEDEPC Year of departure
Format: F4

DATEDEPB Month of departure
Format: F2

DATEDEPA Day of departure
Format: F2

DATEPL Definition of departure
Format: F2

EMBPORT Intended first port of embarkation
Format: F3

ARRPORT Intended port of disembarkation
Format: F3

DESTIN Intended port of return after disembarking slaves
Format: F3

NPPRETRA Number of ports called prior to buying slaves
Format: F1

PLAC1TRA First place of slave purchase
Format: F3

PLAC2TRA Second place of slave purchase
Format: F3

PLAC3TRA Third place of slave purchase
Format: F3

D1SLATRB	Month began slave purchase Format: F2	
D1SLATRA	Day began slave purchase Format: F2	
D1SLATRC	Year began slave purchase Format: F4	
NPAFTTRA	Old World places of call after embarking slaves Format: F3	
DLSLATRB	Month left last slaving port Format: F2	
DLSLATRA	Day left last slaving port Format: F2	
DLSLATRC	Year left last slaving port Format: F4	
NPPRIOR	Number of New World ports of call before disembarkation Format: F1	
SLA1PORT	First port of disembarkation Format: F3	
TSLAVESP	Total slaves purchased Format: F4	
TSLAVESD	Total slaves on board at departure from last slaving port Format: F4	
SLADVOY	Slaves died between last port of purchase and first port of disembarkation Format: F3	
SLAARRIV	Total slaves arrived at first port of disembarkation Format: F4	
DATARR33	Month of first disembarkation of slaves Format: F2	
DATARR32	Day of first disembarkation of slaves Format: F2	
DATARR34	Year of first disembarkation Format: F4	
SLAS32	Slaves disembarked at first port of disembarkation Format: F3	
ADPSALE1	Second port of disembarkation Format: F3	
SLAS36	Slaves disembarked at second port of disembarkation Format: F3	

ADPSALE2	Third port of disembarkation Format: F3
DATARR40	Month of third disembarkation of slaves Format: F2
DATARR39	Day of third disembarkation of slaves Format: F2
SLAS39	Slaves disembarked at third port of disembarkation Format: F3
DDEPAMB	Month of departure from last port of disembarkation Format: F2
DDEPAM	Day of departure from last port of disembarkation Format: F2
DDEPAMC	Year of departure from last port of disembarkation Format: F4
PORTRET	Port at which voyage ended Format: F3
DATARR44	Month in which voyage completed Format: F2
DATARR43	Day on which voyage completed Format: F2
DATARR45	Year in which voyage completed Format: F4
FATE	Outcome of voyage Format: F3
SOURCEA	First source of information Format: A40
SOURCEB	Second source of information Format: A40
SOURCEC	Third source of information Format: A40
SOURCED	Fourth source of information Format: A40
SOURCEE	Fifth source of information Format: A40
SOURCEF	Sixth source of information Format: A40
SOURCEG	Seventh source of information Format: A40
SOURCEH	Eighth source of information Format: A40

SOURCEI	Ninth source of information Format: A40
SOURCEJ	Tenth source of information Format: A40
SOURCEK	Eleventh source of information Format: A40
SOURCEL	Twelfth source of information Format: A40
SOURCEM	Thirteenth source of information Format: A40
SOURCEN	Fourteenth source of information Format: A40
SOURCEO	Fifteenth source of information Format: A40
SOURCEP	Sixteenth source of information Format: A40
SOURCEQ	Seventeenth source of information Format: A40
SOURCER	Eighteenth source of information Format: A40
SLINTEND	Slaves intended from first port of purchase Format: F4
TONNAGE	Tonnage of vessel Format: F4
TONTYPE	Definition of ton used in tonnage Format: F2
NATIONAL	Country in which ship registered Format: F8
CREWDIED	Total crew died on voyage Format: F3
NCAR13	Slaves carried from first port of purchase Format: F3
NCAR15	Slaves carried from second port of purchase Format: F3
NCAR17	Slaves carried from third port of purchase Format: F3
SLADAMER	Slaves died between arrival and sale or release Format: F3
SAILD1	Crew died before first port of purchase Format: F2

SAILD2	Crew died between first slave purchase and departure from last port of purchase Format: F2
SAILD3	Crew died between last slave purchase and first disembarkation point Format: F2
SAILD4	Crew died between first disembarkation of slaves and departure from last port in Americas Format: F2
SAILD5	Crew died after departure from last port of disembarkation Format: F2
NDESERT	Total number of crew deserted Format: F2
EMBPORT2	Second intended port of purchase Format: F3
SLINTEN2	Total slaves intended from second port of purchase Format: F3
GUNS	Number of guns carried Format: F2
VOYAGE	Length of voyage between last port of purchase and first port of disembarkation Format: F3
CREW1	Crew on board at outset of voyage Format: F3
RIG	Rig of vessel Format: F2
CHILD2	Children died on Middle Passage Format: F3
CHILD3	Children at first port of disembarkation Format: F3
PLACCONS	Place of construction Format: F3
YRCONS	Year of construction Format: F4
PLACREG	Place of registration Format: F3
YRREG	Year of registration Format: F4
CREW3	Number of crew at first port of disembarkation Format: F2

CREW4   Number of crew at departure from last port of disembarkation
Format: F2

CREW5   Number of crew at end of voyage
Format: F2

ADULT1   Adults at first port of purchase
Format: F3

CHILD1   Children at first port of purchase
Format: F3

FEMALE1   Females at first port of purchase
Format: F3

MALE1   Males at first port of purchase
Format: F3

MEN1   Men at first port of purchase
Format: F3

WOMEN1   Women at first port of purchase
Format: F3

BOY1   Boys at first port of purchase
Format: F3

GIRL1   Girls at first port of purchase
Format: F3

FEMALE2   Females died on Middle Passage
Format: F3

MALE2   Males died on Middle Passage
Format: F3

MEN2   Men died on Middle Passage
Format: F3

WOMEN2   Women died on Middle Passage
Format: F3

BOY2   Boys died on Middle Passage
Format: F3

GIRL2   Girls died on Middle Passage
Format: F3

MEN3   Men disembarked at first port of disembarkation
Format: F3

WOMEN3   Women disembarked at first port of disembarkation
Format: F3

BOY3   Boys disembarked at first port of disembarkation
Format: F3

GIRL3   Girls disembarked at first port of disembarkation
Format: F3

MALE3	Males disembarked at first port of disembarkation Format: F3
FEMALE3	Females disembarked at first port of disembarkation Format: F3
FEMALE4	Females embarked second port of purchase Format: F3
MALE4	Males embarked at second port of purchase Format: F3
CHILD4	Children embarked at second port of purchase Format: F3
MEN4	Men embarked at second port of purchase Format: F3
WOMEN4	Women embarked at second port of purchase Format: F3
BOY4	Boys embarked at second port of purchase Format: F3
GIRL4	Girls embarked at second port of purchase Format: F3
FEMALE6	Females disembarked at second port of disembarkation Format: F3
MALE6	Males disembarked at second port of disembarkation Format: F3
CHILD6	Children disembarked at second port of disembarkation Format: F3
MEN6	Men disembarked at second port of disembarkation Format: F3
WOMEN6	Women disembarked at second port of disembarkation Format: F3
BOY6	Boys disembarked at second port of disembarkation Format: F3
GIRL6	Girls disembarked at second port of disembarkation Format: F3
CREW2	Crew at departure from last port of slave purchase Format: F3
INFANTM3	Male infants disembarked at first port of disembarkation Format: F3
INFANTF3	Female infants disembarked first port of disembarkation Format: F3
SLADAFRI	Slaves died before departure from last port of purchase Format: F3

SLADIED5	Slaves died during Middle Passage and sale	Format: F3
SLADIED4	Slaves died during purchase and Middle Passage	Format: F3
SLADIED2	Slaves died during purchase, Middle Passage and sale	Format: F3
SLADIED1	Slaves died during unspecified period	Format: F3
SLADIED3	Slaves died because of revolt	Format: F3
SLADIED6	Slaves died during revolt, Middle Passage and sale	Format: F3
INSURREC	Conflict between Africans and Europeans	Format: F1
ADULT3	Adults at first port of disembarkation	Format: F3
DATARR36	Day of arrival at second port of disembarkation	Format: F6
DATARR37	Month of arrival at second port of disembarkation	Format: F6
OWNERA	First owner of venture	Format: A40
OWNERB	Second owner of venture	Format: A40
OWNERC	Third owner of venture	Format: A40
OWNERD	Fourth owner of venture	Format: A40
OWNERE	Fifth owner of venture	Format: A40
OWNERF	Sixth owner of venture	Format: A40
OWNERG	Seventh owner of venture	Format: A40
OWNERH	Eighth owner of venture	Format: A40
OWNERI	Ninth owner of venture	Format: A40
OWNERJ	Tenth owner of venture	Format: A40

OWNERK	Eleventh owner of venture Format: A40
OWNERL	Twelfth owner of venture Format: A40
OWNERM	Thirteenth owner of venture Format: A40
OWNERN	Fourteenth owner of venture Format: A40
OWNERO	Fifteenth owner of venture Format: A40
OWNERP	Sixteenth owner of venture Format: A40

IMPUTED VARIABLES

MAJSELPT	Principal port of slave disembarkation Format: F3
MAJBUYPT	Principal port of slave purchase Format: F3
NATINIMP	Imputed country in which ship registered Format: F2
DEPTREG	Region of departure Format: F2
RETRNREG	Region of return Format: F2
REGISREG	Region of registration Format: F2
YEARAF	Year departed Africa Format: F4
YEARDEP	Year voyage began Format: F4
YEARAM	Year reached port of disembarkation Format: F2
YEAR100	Century in which voyage reached port of disembarkation Format: F4
YEAR5	Quinquennium in which voyage reached port of disembarkation Format: F2
YEAR25	Quarter century in which voyage reached port of disembarkation Format: F2
TONMOD	British measured tons, 1773–1835 Format: F6.1

VYMRTIMP	Imputed deaths of slaves during voyage Format: F8	
TSLMTIMP	Imputed number of slaves on board at outset (for imputing loss) Format: F4	
REGEM1	First region of slave embarkation Format: F2	
REGEM2	Second region of slave embarkation Format: F2	
REGEM3	Third region of slave embarkation Format: F2	
EMBREG	Intended region of first slave embarkation Format: F2	
EMBREG2	Intended region of second slave embarkation Format: F2	
MAJBUYRG	Region in which greatest number of slaves embarked Format: F2	
MAJBYIMP	Imputed region in which greatest number of slaves embarked Format: F2	
REGDIS1	Region of first disembarkation of slaves Format: F2	
REGDIS2	Region of second disembarkation of slaves Format: F2	
REGDIS3	Region of third disembarkation of slaves Format: F2	
REGARRP	Region of intended disembarkation Format: F2	
MAJSELRG	Region in which greatest number of slaves disembarked Format: F2	
FATE2	Fate of voyage from perspective of slaves Format: F1	
FATE3	Fate of voyage from perspective of captor Format: F2	
FATE4	Fate of voyage from perspective of owner Format: F2	
MJSELIMP	Imputed region in which greatest number of slaves disembarked Format: F2	
SLA32IMP	Imputed number of slaves disembarked at first port Format: F4	
SLA36IMP	Imputed number of slaves disembarked at second port Format: F4	

IMPRAT	Proportion of slaves carried to second port of disembarkation Format: F4.2
REGDIS11	Grouping of first regions of disembarkation Format: F4
REGDIS21	Grouping of second region of disembarkation Format: F4
SLA39IMP	Imputed number of slaves disembarked at third region of disembarkation Format: F4
NCR13IMP	Imputed number of slaves embarked at first region of embarkation Format: F4
NCR15IMP	Imputed number of slaves embarked at second region of embarkation Format: F4
NCR17IMP	Imputed number of slaves embarked at third region of embarkation Format: F4
EXPRAT	Proportion of total slaves embarked obtained at first region of embarkation Format: F6.4
MALE1IMP	Imputed number of males embarked Format: F4
FEML1IMP	Imputed number of females embarked Format: F4
CHIL1IMP	Imputed number of children embarked Format: F4
MALRAT1	Proportion of males embarked Format: F6.4
CHILRAT1	Proportion of children embarked Format: F6.4
SLAVEMX1	Total slaves embarked with sex identified Format: F4
SLAVEMA1	Total slaves embarked with age groupings identified Format: F4
MALE3IMP	Imputed numbers of males disembarked Format: F4
FEML3IMP	Imputed number of females disembarked Format: F4
CHIL3IMP	Imputed number of children disembarked Format: F4
MALRAT3	Proportion of males disembarked Format: F6.4

CHILRAT3	Proportion of children disembarked Format: F6.4
SLAVEMX3	Total slaves disembarked with sex identified Format: F4
SLAVEMA3	Total slaves disembarked with age groupings identified Format: F4
ADLT3IMP	Imputed number of adults disembarked Format: F4
VYMRTRAT	Percentage of slaves embarked who died during voyage Format: F6.4
SLAXIMP	Imputed total of slaves embarked Format: F4
SLAMIMP	Imputed total of slaves disembarked Format: F4
DEPTREG1	Imputed region of departure, broadly defined Format: F2
MJSELRG1	Imputed region of disembarkation, broadly defined Format: F2
CONSTREG	Region in which ship was built Format: F2
VOY1IMP	Voyage length: origin (port of departure) to disembarkation of slaves in days Format: F4
VOY2IMP	Voyage length: last port of embarkation to first port of disembarkation Format F4
MALRAT7	Male ratios (either at embarkation or disembarkation—combines MALRAT1 and MALRAT3) Format F7.5
CHILRAT7	Child ratios (either at embarkation or disembarkation—combines CHILRAT1 and CHILRAT3) Format F7.5

Acknowledgments

Research on the trans-Atlantic slave trade has excited much historical controversy, yet this has not prevented scholars from sharing their data. This project would not have been possible in its present form without contributions from a large number of researchers in several countries. The omission of any one of these contributions would have meant that the data set, quite simply, would have included fewer voyages and less complete information. We hope that they are all mentioned in the pages that follow. Just as important, many scholars ensured that the project would find a home, helped it to get funding, and then commented on its interpretative output when this at last began to appear.

Barbara Solow was the moving force that established the project at the W. E. B. Du Bois Institute for Afro-American Research, and did much to ensure its proper funding. She was particularly instrumental in shaping the original concept into a form that was both manageable and sufficiently ambitious in scope. Robert Hall, Jacqueline Goggin, and Patrick Manning gave valuable advice in the critical inaugural meeting of the group and maintained an interest throughout. Randall Burkett, then at the Du Bois Institute, gave us abundant advice on all aspects of the project despite heavy administrative duties and his own numerous original research projects. Together with Carolyn MacLeod, he guided us through the maze that is the Harvard University research funds administrative system. Peter Glenshaw, the Senior Officer, provided us with a wide range of help whenever he was asked.

Johannes Postma gave us his complete set of Dutch voyages in machine-readable form even before we had received funding. Svend E. Holsoe gave us access to his personal archive on the slave trade to the Danish colonies. Joseph E. Inikori provided archival data on the British slave trade from 1764 to 1788. Jerry Handler donated his research notes from the greater part of a career's work on Barbados. From a different career perspective, Jim McMillin was as generous with information collected from late eighteenth-century southern United States newspapers during the preparation of his Ph.D. thesis. James Rawley provided us with his extensive index card collection on London African traders. Joseph C. Miller gave us data on the slave trade to Brazil, 1811–19, and some eighteenth-century French slave trade data collected by Robert L. Stein was also included. Gwendolyn Midlo Hall, Jan Hasselberg, Robin Law, (who drew our attention to the single Norwegian-language reference in the data set), James Pritchard, and John Thornton were assiduous in leading us to sources and voyages that we had overlooked.

Our scholarly output has received critical commentary from a variety of people not directly connected with the project. Ralph Austen encouraged us to begin and has provided astringent criticism on the several papers that we have written with the output of the project. In a similar vein, Stanley L. Engerman has read and commented on, invariably within a day or two of receiving them, and usually again several weeks later, every proposal and paper that the team has written. Selwyn Carrington, Linda Heywood, and other participants at a workshop at Harvard organized by Bernard Bailyn, made useful comments on an early draft of the Introduction. Mary Turner was generous with her expertise (as well as with her house) whenever called upon.

We have been particularly dependent on students. The following have worked as research assistants for the project: Valérie Bada (Université de Liège and Harvard), Steve Bolton and Susan Campbell (both of Queen's University), Lynda Craig (University of Ottawa), Girts Graudins (Harvard), Bob Hall (Queen's University), Neal Losen (University of Northern Iowa), Peter McIsaac (Harvard), Shawn Miller (Columbia University), Peter Pinch (Harvard), Indrani Sen (Hull University), Caroline Sorensen-Gilmour (University of Stirling), Ingrid Stott (Queen's University), Delouis Terlonge (Harvard), Yvonne Tsang (Harvard), Peter Voutov (Harvard), and Patricia Wood (Queen's University). Special appreciation goes to our principal computer programmer, Peter McIsaac, who worked on the project during his own Ph.D. years, coped with its most difficult technical problems almost single-handedly, and deftly juggled the postmodernism of his own research with the dour empiricism of the slave trade project.

Finally, we thank the National Endowment for the Humanities, the Mellon Foundation, the Social Science and Humanities Research Council of Canada, the Ford Foundation, and, for vital seed money, and absorption of some unforeseen expenses at the end, the W. E. B. Du Bois Institute for Afro-American Research, headed by Henry Louis Gates, Jr.